Healing Codependency

How to Resolve Your Childhood that

Creates Relationship Addicts

BY

ELENA MIRO

Copyright Info

© Copyright Elena Miro 2023 - All rights reserved.

The content contained within this book may not be reproduced, duplicated, or transmitted without direct written permission from the author or the publisher except for the use of brief quotations in a book review.

Under no circumstances will any blame or legal responsibility be held against the publisher, or author, for any damages, reparation, or monetary loss due to the information contained within this book. Either directly or indirectly. You are responsible for your own choices, actions, and results.

Legal Notice:

This book is copyright protected. This book is only for personal use. You cannot amend, distribute, sell, use, quote or paraphrase any part, or the content within this book, without the consent of the author or publisher except for the use of brief quotations in a book review.

Disclaimer notice:

Please note the information contained within this book is for educational and entertainment purposes only. All effort has been executed to present accurate, up to date, and reliable, complete information. No warranties of any kind are declared or implied. Readers acknowledge that the author is not engaging in the rendering of legal, financial, medical, or professional advice. The content within this book has been derived from various sources. Please consult a licensed professional before attempting any techniques outlined in this book.

By reading this book, the reader agrees that under no circumstances is the author responsible for any losses, direct or indirect, which are incurred as a result of the use of the information contained within this book, including, but not limited to,—errors, omissions, or inaccuracies.

Table of Contents

BOOK 1

Chapter 1*: The House that Built You and Your Attachment Style*............ 11

Chapter 2*: Childhood Trauma and Human Psychosocial Development* 34

Chapter 3*: The Psychology of Codependency*.. 48

Chapter 4*: The Signs of Relationship Addiction*..................................... 59

Chapter 5*: Your Restless Inner Child* 72

Chapter 6*: Gifts from the Shadows* 82

Chapter 7*: From Denial to Acceptance*.. 95

Chapter 8*: So You're Codependent—What Now?*................................. 105

Chapter 9*: The Road to a Solution – First Steps* 116

BOOK 2

Chapter 1*: Who Built You?*... 124

Chapter 2*: Exploring Within to Heal Throughout*................................... 135

Chapter 3*: Identifying Emotional Triggers and Wounds* 148

Chapter 4*: What Your Inner Child Needs* 164

Chapter 5*: Embrace Your Shadow Self*... 176

Chapter 6*: Becoming Your Own Hero* 189

***Chapter 7**: Resolving Old, Toxic Relationships 206*
***Chapter 8**: The Road to a Happier You 222*
***Chapter 9**: New Habits, New Life... 236*
***Chapter 10**: Keeping It Real 250*

A Word from the Author

For much of my life, I've felt less than whole. I worked hard to try to please the people I loved, but I still didn't feel good about myself. My self-esteem was very low. I felt like I was always on the edge, waiting for one tiny bit of criticism to push me off. What's more, I found that because I didn't value myself, I was neglecting my needs. I always put myself last. At the time, I thought I was just being a good daughter, sister, girlfriend, wife, and so on. I thought I needed to sacrifice myself so others could be happy. It was so ingrained in my personality that I didn't even think of it as a sacrifice; I just thought of it as the standard behavior of someone who loves the people around them. But no matter what I did, I didn't feel like I was a good person. I couldn't understand what else I needed to do. I never thought my problem could be the result of patterns of behavior that began in my childhood. I didn't recognize that it could be the product of childhood trauma. Sure, my family had its share of problems, but nobody physically beat me. I could never have imagined that there are other types of abuse so subtle that you wouldn't even recognize them. I always thought my childhood was okay and sometimes even good. But when I really began delving into my patterns of behavior, I started to see that not everything was as good as I had initially thought. In fact, I came to understand just how dysfunctional my family dynamic had been. Working on my personal growth and experiencing dramatic changes in my life prompted me to pursue a degree in psychology. Now, I want to help other people experience those beneficial changes too.

If any of this resonates with you, you might have the same type of problem that I discovered I have. It's called codependency, and it's an insidious pattern that you develop in childhood and carry into adulthood. It sets you up for failure and can make you a target for abusers. In fact, it's common for codependents to seek out abusers in their life because they recognize them in one way or another. As an adult, you don't often see this pattern in your life. You also don't usually think too much about your childhood and how it might be affecting your life today. But some powerful issues can develop in childhood which could cause even bigger problems as an adult. Do you notice any of the following patterns in your own life today:

- Low self-esteem
- A history of toxic adult relationships
- A strong fear of loneliness
- Problems with addiction (alcohol, drugs, or food)
- A sense of worthlessness
- A strong need to please the people you love so they won't leave you
- A feeling of emptiness that you can't seem to resolve
- Fear of abandonment
- Problems making decisions
- Poor boundaries
- Caretaking behaviors
- Trouble identifying your thoughts, needs, feelings, or desires

If you identify most of these symptoms in yourself, then you might be codependent too. Please note that you are not alone—approximately 50% of the population is codependent. In fact, in one study of over 500 people, 64% of participants showed high levels of codependency. Some estimates suggest that it's possible that more than 90% of the US population exhibits at least some codependent behaviors. This is a very common problem, and it can have a dramatic effect on your quality of life.

I know because it definitely affected my life. I spent a good deal of time studying this problem, both professionally as a psychotherapist and personally as a codependent. I have been through two painful divorces, and I've experienced at least two more codependent relationships. I know how it feels to feel like you desperately need the other people in your life. I also know how it feels to think your childhood was normal until you dig a little deeper and find out that there really were problems. We only have our experience to work from, and until you learn there are other ways of living, it's quite common to idealize the version of childhood that you had. But the kind of childhood that causes codependency can make you terrified of being abandoned. You may become willing to do almost anything someone you love demands so they won't leave you. You feel like you will literally die if they do, but I can also tell you, you won't. There is a way out of this madness. There is a way to live the life of your dreams, have inner freedom, and love without strings of fear attached because you know you're enough by yourself. It took me a long time to find that way out, but I very much want to share what I have learned with you. This book is all about giving you the answers you might not know you're seeking but desperately need. It's about helping you discover the truth so you can move toward a real solution.

That's what I want to share with you in this book; all the ways you can become a people pleaser. I will show you just how your family story and behavioral patterns contributed to your codependency. I will help you understand how your parents shaped your understanding of yourself and your role in life and how the beliefs from your childhood shaped you into the adult you have become. I'll discuss how your psychosocial development was disrupted as a result of the trauma (obvious or not) you endured as a child. I'll examine in-depth the psychology of codependency, the symptoms that indicate you might have this problem, how it would affect your inner child, and how it shapes your view of your shadow self. I'll also help you understand how to move from denial of your problem to acceptance and what you can do once you've reached that important stage. I'll help you toward finding a solution so you can begin healing the trauma. Then, in my second book on this subject—*Healing Codependency: How to Resolve Your Childhood Trauma so You Can Start Living Your Best Life*—I'll take you step-by-step through the healing journey.

These books are filled with helpful exercises for you to use to understand yourself better and find solutions tailored to your situation. I'll talk about the most current research on the subject, what experts have learned through the years about the delicate human psyche, and the many ways it can be harmed. I'll help you recognize what may be subtle clues in your situation that indicate you are codependent. I'll stand beside you as you face that which contributed to the problem in your childhood. I didn't want to believe anything bad about my own mother, but I had to face the painful reality that she was abusive in ways I couldn't see at first.

I'll help you do that too. It's not easy. It takes courage. In fact, it may be the most courageous thing you ever do in your lifetime. It's painful and frightening to look closely into the house that built you, but that's where you must start to truly understand why you are the way you are. Don't worry—I'll be right there with you, and we'll take this journey together. Let's begin by examining your early life story and how that may have shaped your attachment style.

Don't be afraid…together we are strong! Together, we can heal!

Book 1

Am I…..a People Pleaser?

Chapter 1

The House that Built You and Your Attachment Style

We see the world through the lens of our experiences. What happens to us from the moment we are born shapes our psyche and helps to build us into who we will become. For six years, I was in psychotherapy. For many more years, I studied psychology, and I have worked with numerous clients as a psychotherapist. During that time, I was really searching for myself. I was examining the minute details of my own story, my own trauma, and every little thing that made me into the person I am now. It's a journey we all eventually take. It's a struggle to understand why we are the way we are. But sometimes, you need more information to learn just how you came to be and how even the earliest years of your childhood could have had a significant impact on your self-identity. It all begins with how you learn to view the world. That forms the basis for your attachment style and a blueprint for your psychosocial development.

The Early Years and Your Attachment Style

I was not born as a result of love. My mother made this clear to me very early in my life. She never loved my biological father; she loved another man whom she had met years before. He broke her heart, and she never believed she would love again. She told my father that she didn't love him, but he so deeply loved her that he assured her, "My love will be more than enough for the two of us." It might have been enough for the two of them, but it wasn't enough for me. As I said, I was not a baby born of love, and as a result, I was not given the kind of love that would help me form a healthy attachment style. Even as a child, I could sense that somehow, I was not enough. I was also a disappointment to my father, who wanted a boy. Just one more disappointment that even infants can sense.

How do infants sense their parents' emotions? They see in the faces of their parents and feel it in their touch. These visual and physical sensations are how infants experience the world, and that's how they will form their view of what the world is like. Do their parents mirror love with kind, happy, satisfied eyes, or do they display disappointment with apathy or irritation? Children also feel it in touch and embrace, or lack thereof, that conveys those kinds of messages. Is it warm and tender, or cold and clinical? They understand it when they cry and no one comes to help them. This is how they get their initial impression of the world. A preverbal infant has no way of letting someone know they need something other than by crying. When those cries are not answered, they learn that sometimes, their needs may not be met. It teaches them that the world can be an uncaring place.

A man named John Bowlby—a British psychoanalyst—was the first person to attempt to [understand the concept of attachment](). He described the behaviors of infants who were separated from primary caregivers and noted that some infants went to extreme lengths to prevent separation from their parents and reestablish a secure proximity. Many researchers at the time had attributed the distress as the result of immature defense mechanisms, but Bowlby argued that it was an adaptive response shaped by evolutionary forces, given that similar behaviors are often seen in other mammalian species. Like humans, they are dependent upon the adults to care for and protect them until they are developed enough to do so for themselves. Bowlby argued that those with a more secure attachment would be more likely to survive to reproductive age, which explains how natural selection likely shaped the attachment behavioral system.

Attachment Styles Defined

While Bowlby recognized the attachment dynamics, it was his colleague, Mary Ainsworth, who did the experiments that allowed her to identify individual differences in attachment styles. She separated 12-month-old infants from their parents, and then observed their reactions when they were reunited. She found that there were three basic styles:

❖ Secure Attachment Style

The children with this attachment style exhibited what Bowlby called **normative behavior**. They were upset when separated from their parents, but when the parent returned, they sought them out and were easily comforted by them. About 60% of the children who participated in the experiments were identified as having a secure attachment style.

❖ Anxious-Resistant Attachment Style

Some, about 20% or fewer, of the children who participated in the experiments were found to have what came to be called an **anxious-resistant** attachment style. These children were ill-at-ease in the strange setting of the laboratory, but when they were separated from their parents, they became extremely distressed. Once reunited with their parents, it was still difficult to soothe them, and they exhibited conflicting behaviors that indicated that, although they wanted to be comforted, they also wanted to punish their parents for leaving.

❖ Avoidant Attachment Style

Another 20% of children exhibited an **avoidant** attachment style. These children did not appear very distressed when separated from their parents. When they were reunited, they actively *avoided* seeking contact with the parent, in contrast with the previous attachment styles we discussed.

❖ Disorganized/Disoriented Attachment Style:

Since those early experiments by Ainsworth, other researchers identified another attachment style in 1986. This is the **disorganized/disoriented** or **fearful-avoidant** attachment style. Like the other insecure attachment styles, it stems from childhood trauma or neglect. Individuals with this attachment style feel like they don't deserve love or closeness. They never learned to self-soothe as children, and as a result, they feel confused and unsettled in relationships as they experience emotional extremes. These would be the children in Ainsworth's study who exhibited a mixture of behaviors associated with both anxious-resistant and avoidant attachment styles.

Perhaps the most important finding from Ainsworth's and Main and Solomon's research was that the individual differences in attachment style correlated with interactions between the infant and their parents during the first year of life at home. Many people had presumed that children that young were not affected by their environment and interactions because they couldn't remember it. Ainsworth's research showed that, in fact, even an infant is taking in their experiences and forming beliefs about the world. The children who were more secure in their attachment styles had parents who were responsive to their needs, whereas the children who exhibited the other two styles had parents who were insensitive to their needs. They may have been inconsistent in their responses, or they may have outright rejected their responsibilities in providing for the infant.

My experience during the first two years of my life was one of rejection and insensitivity. My own mother stopped breastfeeding me at two weeks of age. She had no reason for doing so, but later said it was because my father was unsupportive of her needs. At six months old, my mother was already pregnant with my brother, around that time when her mother died. She was distracted from caring for her infant daughter, to say the least. Her attention was on her mother's death and the child growing inside her. My brother was born a heavy child, and during childbirth, both my mother's and brother's lives were at risk. In fact, the doctor told my father that he had to choose which of them they should save. Fortunately, an experienced midwife saved them both, but it became increasingly apparent that my brother's life was considered more valuable than mine.

Of course, mothers may have a special relationship with their sons and a more complicated one with their daughters, but my mother placed some big demands on me at a very young age. When I was just one year and two months old, she focused on my brother's needs, and my needs fell to a distant second place. I was clearly not her priority, and even a child of such a young age can sense that in a primary caregiver. My mother continuously reinforced that message as I grew older. While my brother and I grew up close and spent lots of time together until our lives took us in different directions, I always felt the weight of my mother's preference for my brother. At a very young age, I was already feeling like I wasn't good enough. I was more of an attendant and less of a beloved child, and this all occurred during the first two years of my life. I can say it definitely affected my attachment style.

Attachment Style Manifesting in Adulthood

The attachment style patterns you develop in your first years tend to persist into adulthood. How you view the world—as a relatively safe place where your needs will be met most of the time, or as a dangerous place where your needs might not be met—greatly affects the behavior patterns you develop as you grow into adulthood. Likewise, these patterns affect the types and nature of the close relationships you form with others. Here are the types of behaviors seen with the different styles.

Secure Attachment Style

Infants with a secure attachment style tend to grow into well-adjusted, resilient children who are well-liked and get along with their peers. As adults, they are more satisfied in their relationships, which are characterized by greater longevity, commitment, and trust. They could also be described as interdependent, which means they use their romantic partners as a secure base from which they can explore the world. When distressed, they are more likely than an insecure adult to seek comfort from their partner. They are also more likely to give support to their partner when distressed. Moreover, the attributions they make concerning their partner's behavior when they're in conflict tend to alleviate any insecurity. The opposite is true of adults with insecure attachment styles. They make attributions that exacerbate their insecurities.

Insecure Attachment Styles

The two insecure attachment styles (Anxious and Avoidant) involve behaviors that include ambivalence, resistance, and withdrawal. In a way, the child is trying to minimize feelings of attachment and the behaviors that go along with that. They are trying to avoid the pain of having someone they love or need be ripped away from them. They don't want to seem vulnerable. This is confirmed by the research showing that biologically, avoidant children who exhibit behaviors of ambivalence toward their parents following separation are actually experiencing stress. Their heart rate and stress hormone levels are all elevated, even if they appear as cool as a cucumber.

As adults, such individuals are poorly adjusted. Although they can become distressed upon losing someone they love, they are effectively able to dismiss their thoughts and feelings about the loss. They could, in a sense, deactivate their psychological responses to a degree by distracting themselves from attachment-related thoughts. As you might imagine, these individuals come across to their partners as less caring. Additionally, although they can suppress their feelings of losing someone they love, that can create worse problems for themselves in the long run. Insecure attachment styles also result in obsessive behaviors designed to minimize the likelihood of loss. Conflicting emotions and adaptive responses create a kind of push-me-pull-me effect. These individuals are constantly pushing the people they love away, but when they drift too far away, they pull them back in. Of course, extreme attachment disorders can result in a variety of mental disorders, as we've seen through studies.

What Does Attachment Have to Do with Codependency?

So, at an early age, I was neglected by my mother and given responsibilities beyond my years. The latter is often referred to as parentification by the experts, and both of those early childhood experiences are contributing factors to the formation of codependency. But the causes of codependency are multifactorial; various contributors include biological, psychological, and social elements. What's more, codependency can be placed on a spectrum of severity, from excessive feminine (i.e., caretaking) behavior, to that of a behavioral addiction, and all the way to a psychopathological personality disorder. Originally associated with women who, although appearing to dominate their partners, were actually dependent on their spouses, it has come to be recognized as a problem that both men and women can have. Moreover, its occurrence is not just limited to the context of a romantic relationship, and additionally, it's not something that is only the result of early childhood experiences. It can also develop from changes in perception of a woman's role in a sociocultural context, as well as the emergence of a substance abuse problem within the family unit.

Some studies have indicated that children who grow up in homes full of parental conflict—that with alcohol involved or not—can develop codependency in later stages of life. These children learn to put their focus outside of themselves. They learn not to express their feelings for fear of triggering a dysfunctional response from an abusive parent. Furthermore, they embrace the role of "helper" or "savior" within the family. This can easily disrupt their identity development, and as adults, it often creates issues with their partners that can even be viewed as "addictive." As children, they often have attempted to resolve conflicts they witnessed between their parents. They have taken it upon themselves to keep the peace in the family and frequently develop an insecure attachment style that promotes overly dependent interpersonal relationships. What's more, they give up their individual autonomy to serve the needs of the group, which can easily lead to a misrepresentation of reality. They also exhibit poor emotional regulation and insufficient interpersonal communication patterns.

Despite the plethora of symptoms, codependency frequently remains unrecognized. Codependents often enter the health care system complaining of stress-related and depressive symptoms, with the underlying factors remaining invisible. The patient doesn't recognize their own symptoms, nor do they necessarily think that their childhood was in any way problematic. They may see it as normal, since they wouldn't have anything to compare it with.

This was my situation. As part of my child-like adaptive strategy to protect myself from harm, I had convinced myself that my father's acceptance that my mother could never love him was romantic. He loved her that much, despite her love for another man, combined with how he wanted a boy, it all added to my early impression that I was not enough. Still, I grew up thinking my childhood was okay. I wasn't really harmed. Oh, how wrong I was. I didn't see any of the hidden trauma and underlying scars that were accumulating in my life.

My Attachment Style

My attachment style formed when my needs were not met as an infant. Your attachment style forms before you're three years old; in those early years, I could sense my mother's distance, and when she stopped breastfeeding me at only two weeks of age, I learned that sometimes, my need for warmth and closeness might not be met. When my mother became pregnant with my brother and her mother died when I was around six months old, I sensed her distraction and sadness. I also understood at 14 months old that my brother's life and happiness were a clear priority over mine. These experiences contributed to my anxious-avoidant attachment style. As I continued to grow, the experiences of my family life only served to confirm that the world was a dangerous place that didn't care for, nor prioritize, my needs.

I was a calm child and a good girl, but when I was around five to six years old, the Soviet Union collapsed. This was not an easy time for my parents, and at the age of six, we had moved to another town. This is the moment that I later came to realize was when I changed into a shy child who was more reserved and withdrawn. Of course, I had to go to a new school where I didn't know anyone. It was October when we moved, and since it was cold, we weren't allowed to go outside for recess. Thus, I didn't have a chance to make friends on the playground. I was a curious child, so I read a lot.

By the time it was warm again and we could play outside, I hadn't made any real friends, so I was always alone and reading on the balcony. I did finally make a good friend—a girl with whom I could share my secrets and talk about anything—but that wasn't meant to last long. When I was 12 years old, my mother enrolled me in the best humanitarian school in our small town. Once again, I had no one, and once again, I became shy and reserved. Over time, though, I made friends, even though I was never really an excellent student like my mother had been when she was young. That was something she constantly reminded me of, and it was yet another message to say that I simply didn't measure up in her eyes.

Still, I didn't see her behavior as abuse. For me, it was normal. I was proud of my mother's accomplishments in her life, and I loved her. I thought she was the best mother a person could have. I was idealizing her and ignoring her conditional love. When I got good grades, she seemed to love me, but when I didn't, I could see the disappointment in her eyes. I remember when I was around eight or nine years old, I got pretty bad grades in math, and I knew I would have to go home and face her withering disapproval. I was so sad that I began crying, and I continued crying for hours until I became sick; from there, I got a headache and developed a fever. My shame was manifesting itself in physical symptoms. Somewhere in my psyche, I knew that my mother wouldn't berate me for my bad grades if she saw how much I was suffering. She would, in fact, dedicate herself to caring for me, and that would make me feel special. I remember going to the hospital and feeling so important because it was just her and me there. She was loving and kind, as opposed to her normal way of being—cold, distant, and critical. The somatization I experienced as a result of my emotional distress became my exotic way of avoiding being shamed by my mother for my failures. She believed that criticism was what made a person better, so that's what I remember most from my mother. It was never her support, kind words, or compliments. Then again, I didn't know any better. She was my mother, and like all kids, I saw her as a kind of god that could not be defied or criticized. I tried so hard to be the best so I could get her kind attention, as opposed to her criticism. I wanted her to notice something good in me. I wanted her to see that I was worthy of love.

You can probably see why I developed an insecure attachment style. The early life neglect, combined with a persistent reinforcement of that feeling of neglect left me uncertain of my own worth. My mother's love was conditional, and no matter how hard I worked to please her, I couldn't live up to her expectations. The world did, indeed, feel like a dangerous place that wouldn't provide for my needs.

My mother also groomed me as the helper of the family. My job was to care for my brother at an early age, and I took it upon myself to care for my mother as well. I was constantly hoping that she would recognize my worth and give me the unconditional love I so desperately wanted. This was all part of my developing codependency, and these experiences build upon each other to create a pattern of behavior. At a young age, my pattern was already taking shape.

What About Your Attachment Style?

This is something you might be experiencing as well. You're looking for something, but you aren't even sure what it is. You feel empty, so you question your worth. You want validation, but you don't seem to find it anywhere you look. You want someone to need you, to believe that what you have to offer is a gift they want in their life. You constantly worry about disappointing the people you love because, somewhere deep inside, you are certain that you will eventually. You doubt your abilities, and you invest your time in helping others prove your worth. These are all red flags, but let's dig a little deeper—let's see what lies beneath the surface of these sentiments.

Exercise #1

Reflections on Attachment

In this chapter, I've reflected on some of my childhood experiences and how those contributed to my attachment style and, ultimately, my codependency. Now, I want you to do the same. I have created an exercise to get at the roots of some of your beliefs about yourself and how those might relate to your attachment style. From there, we'll look at the nature of childhood trauma and how it affects psychosocial development. But first, let's do an exercise to identify your attachment style.

Consider the following statements from the time of your earliest childhood memories and rate your experience on a scale of 1 to 5, with 1 being never and 5 being always:

I felt safe with my mother.

Never	Rarely	Sometimes	Usually	Always
1	2	3	4	5

I felt safe with my father.

Never	Rarely	Sometimes	Usually	Always
1	2	3	4	5

My mother encouraged me to explore the world and find my natural talents.

Never	Rarely	Sometimes	Usually	Always
1	2	3	4	5

My father encouraged me to explore the world and find my natural talents.

Never	Rarely	Sometimes	Usually	Always
1	2	3	4	5

My mother was physically present while I was growing up.

Never	Rarely	Sometimes	Usually	Always
1	2	3	4	5

My father was physically present while I was growing up.

Never	Rarely	Sometimes	Usually	Always
1	2	3	4	5

My parents provided for my basic needs (food, housing, and medical care).

Never	Rarely	Sometimes	Usually	Always
1	2	3	4	5

When I was distressed, my parents recognized my distress and made me feel as though they understood how I was feeling.

Never	Rarely	Sometimes	Usually	Always
1	2	3	4	5

When I was distressed, my parents soothed me and calmed me down.

Never	Rarely	Sometimes	Usually	Always
1	2	3	4	5

My parents expressed interest and delight in who I was, and they made me feel valued and loved.

Never	Rarely	Sometimes	Usually	Always
1	2	3	4	5

My parents gave me the material things I wanted to have.

Never	Rarely	Sometimes	Usually	Always
1	2	3	4	5

My parents took me to do the things I wanted to do (activities, visiting friends, etc.)

Never	Rarely	Sometimes	Usually	Always
1	2	3	4	5

I feel comfortable expressing my feelings to my mother (if deceased, rate it based on how you felt when she was alive).

Never	Rarely	Sometimes	Usually	Always
1	2	3	4	5

I feel comfortable expressing my feelings to my father (if deceased, rate it based on how you felt when he was alive).

Never	Rarely	Sometimes	Usually	Always
1	2	3	4	5

I find my mother to be a dependable person.

Never	Rarely	Sometimes	Usually	Always
1	2	3	4	5

I find my father to be a dependable person.

Never	Rarely	Sometimes	Usually	Always
1	2	3	4	5

It helps to turn to my mother in times of need.

Never	Rarely	Sometimes	Usually	Always
1	2	3	4	5

It helps to turn to my father in times of need.

Never	Rarely	Sometimes	Usually	Always
1	2	3	4	5

I worry that my mother doesn't really care for me.

Never	Rarely	Sometimes	Usually	Always
1	2	3	4	5

I worry that my father doesn't really care for me.

Never	Rarely	Sometimes	Usually	Always
1	2	3	4	5

I worry that my mother will abandon me.

Never	Rarely	Sometimes	Usually	Always
1	2	3	4	5

I worry that my father will abandon me.

Never	Rarely	Sometimes	Usually	Always

1	2	3	4	5

Now, time for some reflection: First, add up your score. If you scored 22 - 66, you might have an insecure attachment style. If your score was more than 66, you probably have a secure attachment style. Of course, it would require some work with a therapist to truly understand the nature of your attachment style; a simple test like this can't possibly cover the range of behaviors related to this field. But these questions should give you a rough idea of your basic style. At least, it's a place to reflect on your patterns.

In a personal journal, reflect on your answers. What experiences in your childhood might have made you feel this way? Can you remember specific incidents? Elaborate as much as you like on your answers and the emotions that these memories bring up for you.

Now, let's turn to your romantic partner. If you don't have a current romantic partner, respond to the statements regarding your most recent romantic partner. If you have never had a romantic partner, imagine how you would feel (be brutally honest) about these statements.

I feel comfortable expressing my feelings to this person.

Never	Rarely	Sometimes	Usually	Always
1	2	3	4	5

I find this person to be dependable.

Never	Rarely	Sometimes	Usually	Always
1	2	3	4	5

It helps to turn to this person in times of need.

Never	Rarely	Sometimes	Usually	Always
1	2	3	4	5

I never question whether they care for me—I know they do.

Never	Rarely	Sometimes	Usually	Always
1	2	3	4	5

I never worry about this person abandoning me.

Never	Rarely	Sometimes	Usually	Always
1	2	3	4	5

I can easily calm myself after an argument with this person.

Never	Rarely	Sometimes	Usually	Always
1	2	3	4	5

I can easily show how I'm feeling deep down to this person.

Never	Rarely	Sometimes	Usually	Always
1	2	3	4	5

I know I deserve the love this person gives me.

Never	Rarely	Sometimes	Usually	Always
1	2	3	4	5

Some more scores—add up what you got in this section. If you scored between 8 and 24, that might indicate you don't feel secure in your attachment to this person. Scores above 24 indicate more security in your attachment to your romantic partner. Now, reflect on each of the questions and what they mean. For example, if you answered that you struggle knowing whether you deserve the love this person gives you, what does that say about your concept of self-worth? Why do you think you feel that way? What experiences made you feel that way? Did someone in your life tell you that you don't deserve to be loved? What about your trust in this person—do you trust them, or do you worry about whether they really care about you? Have they given you a reason to distrust them, for example? Can you soothe yourself after an argument with them, or do you want them to comfort you?

People with a secure attachment style generally find it easier to open up to other people and trust them. They are not overly worried about being abandoned, and they feel confident enough in themselves to share their feelings with others. The people in their lives upon whom they were dependent provided for their basic needs, at least most of the time, and were genuinely interested in them. They were present, loving, and soothing when problems arose. They were someone with whom they felt safe. If your answers don't reflect those basic attitudes, it's possible that you have an insecure attachment style, as

I do. Again, I would recommend you work with a therapist to uncover the truth about your attachment style and the trauma that created it—but this is still a place to start. If you do appear to have an insecure attachment style, that could lead to codependency or other problems within your relationships and life. It will certainly affect how you view the world in general. But now that you understand more about your attachment style and how it might affect you, you can be better able to deal with your emotions. Let's examine now how childhood trauma can affect your psychosocial development—that's an important part of how you became you.

Chapter 2

Childhood Trauma and Human Psychosocial Development

By now, you may have started to notice some of the elements of my childhood that created an anxious attachment style. I was neglected in my early years, and I was also then parentified—given responsibilities beyond my years when I had to care for my brother. I was constantly criticized and denied unconditional love, which would build a child's self-esteem and encourage healthy identity development. I tried to please my mother, but I was constantly failing to live up to her expectations. These experiences had a dramatic effect on the development of my identity—that is, how I see myself.

This is true for any child. Your experiences early in life will affect how you view your identity and place in the world. Can you identify some of your experiences that affected your development? These will likely be tied to strong memories you have from your younger years. These experiences are foundational for the development of personality, and they are solidly grounded in psychological theory. It's important to understand human psychosocial development theories to understand what happens when things don't proceed healthily.

Erikson's Stages of Human Psychosocial Development

Erik Erikson was a German psychologist who is now considered one of the most influential psychologists of the 20th century. His work in personality development was particularly important. Erikson believed that our personalities develop in a predetermined order through eight stages. These psychosocial development stages occur from infancy through adulthood. In each stage, an individual is faced with a psychosocial crisis, and how that crisis is dealt with can result in a positive or negative outcome. These eight stages, the basic virtues they create if there is a positive outcome, and the age at which they occur are presented in the table below.

Erikson's Eight Stages of Human Psychosocial Development

Stage	Psychosocial Crisis	Basic Virtue	Age
1.	Trust vs. Mistrust	Hope	0 - 1½
2.	Autonomy vs. Shame	Will	1½ - 3

3.	Initiative vs. Guilt	Purpose	3 - 5
4.	Industry vs. Inferiority	Competency	5 - 12
5.	Identity vs. Role Confusion	Fidelity	12 - 18
6.	Intimacy vs. Isolation	Love	18 - 40
7.	Generativity vs. Stagnation	Care	40 - 65
8.	Ego Integrity vs. Despair	Wisdom	65+

By understanding what happens in each stage and the possible positive or negative outcomes, you can see how problems in one stage might leave you with certain behavioral patterns, including codependency. Specifically, failure in stages 1, 2, or 3 can result in codependent behavioral patterns, and when you combine that with an insecure attachment style, it makes the likelihood of developing a dependent personality much greater. In my case, my mother was not available to tend to my needs as a newborn. She lost her own mother when I was six months old. Even as an infant, I sensed her sorrow. As a result of her own pain, she was not as responsive to my needs, leaving me to believe that the world was not safe. But I was also left with the trauma of rejection. This kind of trauma forms when you believe people don't care about you or don't love you despite your need or love for them. This early experience caused me to fail to achieve hope in stage 1. Instead, I started to mistrust that my needs would be met, resulting in an insecure (anxious-avoidant) attachment style. This is what ultimately created my form of codependency. I need a lot of love and intimacy from other people, since I didn't get that from my mother. Similarly, I also fell into a pattern of quitting before I got fired out of my fear of rejection, meaning the issue started to leak into other parts of my life.

Stage 1

Trust vs. Mistrust

This is the stage that typically forms your attachment style, as we've discussed. As an infant, you don't know the world yet. You're like an explorer on a distant planet, completely dependent on a caregiver for all your needs. If you get consistent, predictable, and reliable care, you develop a sense of trust. That gives you a strong foundation of security when dealing with challenges later in life. Even if threatened, you will believe you can manage it. A big part of that is developing a virtue of hope. With hope, you can see a better day coming and a better way forward, and you know that you can find that path.

If, on the other hand, you don't get consistent, predictable, or reliable care at this stage, you become fearful. You mistrust your relationships, develop anxiety, feel insecure, and view the world as a more dangerous place. This ties into Bowlby's research on attachment because, with a basic sense of mistrust, you could find it more difficult to develop strong attachments. You don't trust that other people will be there for you and help you. Failing to develop trust at this stage doesn't always mean you've been actively abused by a caregiver. It can happen as a result of neglect or due to processes that are beyond your caregiver's control.

For example, one woman I know was in and out of the hospital during the first two years of her life. This was during a time when her parents were only allowed to visit during visiting hours, which were limited at that time for infants. Moreover, during this time, she was being treated for pneumonia and bronchitis, so she was experiencing a very frightening, unpredictable, painful, and confusing experience as an infant. All she knew was that no one was holding her lovingly very often or consistently, and she was being hurt by needles or other medical equipment. To her, the world was indeed unpredictable, frightening, and painful. While her mother visited her every chance she got and was very loving when she did, it wasn't consistent enough to be predictable. Thus, she developed an insecure attachment style, which naturally bled into her adult relationships.

State 2

Autonomy vs. Shame

This stage of psychosocial development occurs between 18 months and approximately 3 years. It is during this time that a child learns to develop a sense of personal control over their physical abilities, as well as a sense of independence. It's also during this stage that your attachment style forms. If you can do this successfully, you will develop a virtue of will, which will help you become more confident and secure in your abilities. The key to success is if your caregiver encourages you to become independent and supports you in that effort. Although they may let you fail occasionally, the key is that they support and encourage you to try again. They also allow you to be more independent by letting you, for example, walk away from them more, make choices about what you wear, and decide what you eat. They protect you from constant failure, but they also let you learn that you can come back from failure too. If a child's caregivers are critical and overly controlling, or if they prevent them from asserting themselves, the child will come to doubt their abilities. That can cause them to become overly dependent on other people. They will also lack self-esteem and can develop a sense of shame about their inability to do things for themselves.

Stage 3

Initiative vs. Guilt

This stage occurs when the child is about three to five years old, and it is a very rapid period of development. The child is now interacting with other children at school and are playing regularly, which gives them an opportunity to explore their interpersonal skills and initiate activities. They approach and interact with other children, plan activities, and invent games. If they are allowed and encouraged to do this, they will start to gain some confidence in leading others and making decisions for themselves. They develop a sense of initiative. This stage is also when the child will be asking numerous—seemingly endless—questions, and if the caregiver answers them with patience, they are offering a healthy learning environment to the child about the world around them.

Failure in this stage can occur in a number of ways. If a primary caregiver discourages the child's activities and interactions with other children, either due to criticism or from overly controlling their activities, the child will then develop a sense of guilt. Often, a child's behavior during this stage is seen as overly aggressive by a parent, the latter of whom may then punish the child or restrict their activities. This is one way they can cause the child to feel that needless guilt. Additionally, if the caregiver dismisses their questions as stupid, trivial, or embarrassing, the child will feel further guilty and ashamed. With too much guilt, a child's creativity can be inhibited.

Note that some guilt is necessary for the child to learn self-control and have a conscience, but there needs to be a balance. If the child has the right amount of balance between initiative and guilt, then they can feel a purpose, whereas failure can cause an unhealthy amount of guilt.

Stage 4

Industry (Competence) vs. Inferiority

This stage happens between ages five and 12 years old, and it's when children typically learn to read and write, so sums, among other things on their own. Teachers become increasingly more important in the child's life, as do peer groups, and these influences become a major part of how the child builds self-esteem. They want the approval of these people, and they seek it out by demonstrating their competency in performing certain skills. If they can perform well and appropriately according to their peers, family, and teachers, they can gain some pride and more confidence in what they've accomplished.

If their caregiver encourages them and reinforces their initiative, they will start to feel competent or even industrious. They come to believe they can achieve their goals. If they are restricted by parents or teachers, then they will start to doubt their abilities, which can then cause them to not reach their potential. By failing to develop the skills required to be successful in society, they will then start feeling inferior. A little failure can help a child develop modesty, but too much can make them feel incompetent.

Stage 5

Identity vs. Role Confusion

Between 12 to 18 years old, an adolescent starts developing their identity. They are now trying to determine their personal values, beliefs, and goals while transitioning from childhood to adulthood. They are becoming increasingly independent and trying to determine what they want to do with their lives. Do they want a family? What kind of career do they want? How will they fit into society? What will their role be? How they go about answering these questions will end up guiding their ethical development. A healthy outcome for the end of this stage is an integrated sense of self and an understanding of who they are and what they want to be. Success means they grow into the maturational changes that occur in adolescence and are able to accept themselves for who they are. They can also commit to others and accept them, even if there are ideological differences between them, as well as start to take their place in society. Being able to do these things requires the virtue of fidelity.

Of course, to develop their identity, they must explore their possibilities, which means they must be given the freedom to do so by caregivers. Excessive pressure into building a particular identity can result in rebellion, which may then take the form of establishing an unhealthy identity. Without the freedom to explore their environment and opportunities, they may become confused about their role in life. This can make them uncertain about their worth, which can ultimately lead to an unhappy future. Additionally, the failure to develop that sense of identity can lead to numerous psychopathologies, including narcissistic personality disorder and borderline personality disorder. It can cause an individual to have to seek out other people if they want to find their identity, thus eventually leading to a life of dependency on others.

Stage 6

Intimacy vs. Isolation

This stage occurs in the prime of life—that is, between the ages of 18 and 40 years old. The conflict that happens during this time is usually centered around forming loving relationships with other people. People in this age range share themselves more intimately with others while exploring relationships that might lead to long-term commitments outside of the family. If an individual is successful and able to be intimate with others, they can form happy relationships based on commitment, safety, and mutual care. On the other hand, if they are unable to get close to others, then they come to fear commitment and may be unable to form long-lasting, healthy relationships. This can lead to isolation, loneliness, and other problems like depression and anxiety. Success during this stage is imperative to ensure loving and healthy relationships.

Stage 7

Generativity vs. Stagnation

This stage occurs between the age of 40 and 65 years old, and it is a period often called "making your mark." This is when people think about how they will be remembered and what they will leave behind. People in this stage often wish to nurture or create something they consider meaningful and beneficial to other people. These are the things people will remember about them. It's a way to give back to the world. You might do this by raising good children, becoming successful in your career, and/or getting involved with your community. Generativity means that the person feels like they are a part of something bigger than themselves. They feel useful and accomplished, leading to the virtue of care. If they are not successful, they feel stagnant, unproductive, and as though they only have a shallow connection to the world around them. They feel disconnected and uninvolved with their community and their culture.

Stage 8

Ego Integrity vs. Despair

Erikson's final stage of psychosocial development begins at age 65 and ends with death. This is when an individual contemplates their accomplishments, reflects on their life, takes note of any regrets, and, if successful, accepts their life as something that was meant to be. This makes them feel coherent and whole, knowing they led a successful life. Their productivity at this stage slows down, and they can retire in peace. As they have developed the virtue of wisdom, they believe they can die without fear. Although they may occasionally feel some despair, it is balanced by their ego integrity and doesn't overcome them. On the other hand, if a person feels unproductive, guilty about what they've done in their past, or that they didn't accomplish the things they wanted to do in life, they may feel a profound despair that they cannot overcome. They will be dissatisfied with their life, which can lead to depression and hopelessness, given that there's little they believe they can do about it all now.

Back to My Story

From my story so far, it's easy to see that I experienced mistrust in Stage 1 due to my mother's critical nature and tendency to control and saddle me with too much responsibility. Given this state of affairs, it is logical that I rebelled in my teenage years. While my parents were merely okay together, they did have their fights. I always sided with my mother, of course, because I saw my father as someone who wasn't as good as her. I thought he should feel lucky that she was with him. Well, maybe that message had been transmitted to me over the years from my mother.

But he worked very hard to take care of our family and live up to my mother's expectations. After all, he was working under the burden of knowing that she didn't really love him, so I can't blame him for wanting to imagine a different reality or avoid it altogether from time to time. He would go out with his friends and really tie one on. Usually, when this happened, my mother would welcome him home with a veritable deluge of accusations and comments about morality and how he wasn't demonstrating any. They would often fight for half the night. Of course, my mother always painted herself as a victim, martyr, and saint, and I always took her side. In fact, I loved her even more when she was complaining about my father. As a child, I had seen him as a terrible man, but that was the drama created in my family, often by my mother herself.

On one occasion, my mother didn't get up and fight with my father when he came home drunk. Instead, she pretended to be asleep as a way of punishing him with her silence and indifference. He was a man who wanted her acceptance, love, and respect, so he would get lonely without any response from her. He decided to take a bath to calm himself, but he fell asleep in the tub. A few days later, he became ill with bilateral pneumonia. He was hospitalized and treated for more than a year, and although he survived, he was always weak after that experience, and after, he was ultimately diagnosed with liver cancer and only lived for seven more years. It was during my teenage years that he was in the hospital, always hovering between life and death. During his treatment and after he died, our family suffered financially since my mother's salary was so low, making it very difficult to survive. We often didn't even have enough money for food, and we additionally had to pay the medical bills for my father.

As you might imagine, my mother was constantly irritated by this situation. She was moody and quick to fly into a rage. I couldn't even find refuge at school. We didn't have enough money for clothing and shoes, so I was ridiculed for my appearance by my peers. It was a really tough time for all of us. By the time I was ready to enter the university, I couldn't wait to get away from this terrible, small town and the tyranny of my mother's abuse. She constantly made accusations and devalued me. I was yearning to be free and independent. What's more, when I was 16 years old, I had a terrible experience that would affect my ability to develop intimate, long-lasting, committed relationships, but I will elaborate on that in the next chapter. Right now, let's talk about you.

Exercise #2

How Did You Do in Each Stage?

This exercise will help you reflect on how you fared in these stages of psychosocial development. Begin by answering the following questions, but be aware that you may experience a variety of emotions while doing so. You may feel rage, sadness, fear, among many other emotions that you might not expect. This is why it's vital that you take care of yourself throughout the process. Be kind to yourself, particularly if you uncover certain memories where a caregiver may have failed you. Remember that no matter what you experienced, you survived, and you are stronger and more resilient than you realize because of it. Make sure you have someone you love and who has your best interests at heart ready to respond to a call for help. Also, make sure you treat yourself with the kindness, love, and respect you deserve. With that in mind, let's proceed. After each question, elaborate and reflect on your thoughts, experiences, and emotions in your journal. Remember, there are no wrong answers here; this exercise is for self-exploration, so be honest with yourself.

- **Question #1:** What do you know about your infancy? Were your caregivers present, or were there periods of separation?
- **Question #2:** Do you feel a need to always develop a contingency plan when making decisions? In other words, do you need a Plan A, Plan B, Plan C, etc.?
- **Question #3:** Do you fear that you will have needs that won't be met? Has this ever happened to you?
- **Question #4:** Do you often feel helpless? What kinds of situations make you feel helpless?
- **Question #5:** Do strange situations or environments frighten and make you retreat?
- **Question #6:** Do you like to travel to places you've never been to before?
- **Question #7:** Do you believe that you make a positive contribution to your family, community, and culture?
- **Question #8:** If someone you love is better at something than you are, do you feel proud of them?
- **Question #9:** Do you feel proud when you can do something well?
- **Question #10:** Do you know your role in society?
- **Question #11:** Are you confident that you know who you are, what your values are, and what your beliefs are?
- **Question #12:** Are you comfortable being vulnerable around someone you love?

The following questions are for people over 40 years of age.

- **Question #13:** What are some things you've done in your life that you believe are beneficial to others?
- **Question #14:** In what ways do you make positive contributions to your community?
- **Question #15:** Are you a good friend?

The following questions are for people over 65 years of age.

- **Question #16:** Do you have any regrets? If so, what are they?
- **Question #17**: What accomplishments are you most proud of?
- **Question #18:** Do you believe the things that happened in your life happened for a reason?
- **Question #19:** Do you believe the challenges you faced in life made you stronger?
- **Question #20:** If you were to die today, would you feel like you had done everything you came here to do?

Once you have answered these questions, take a look at your answers and what they say about the different stages of your life. How do you think you fared in each stage of psychosocial development? What kinds of experiences affected your outcomes in each stage? Reflect on these findings in your journal and be sure to treat yourself to an act of kindness after you finish this exercise. Go do something you like, eat something you love, and show yourself a little love. Now that you have a better understanding of your development, let's look a little deeper into the psychology of codependency.

Chapter 3

The Psychology of Codependency

I was 16 years old, and my life was in a constant state of chaos. My father was hovering between life and death, and my mother was constantly irritated. School was a nightmare, where I was ridiculed for my appearance and how I never had enough money for me to dress to the standards of my peers. I felt awkward and unaccepted everywhere I turned. No matter how hard I tried, I couldn't seem to please anyone—well, almost anyone. There was a man, the director of our gymnasium, who showered me with affection. He was 50 years old and always all smiles and compliments. He was flirting, but I didn't see it as a young, naive girl. I get it now, but at the time, I didn't know. He seemed at times to be my only friend, and I was starved for affection. This man wanted me to go to one of the best universities in our country. He even met my mother to convince her to support me in applying to this university. Well, she decided that he was attracted to her, and her eyes had quite the shine when she told me about it. She was practically gushing. The problem was, it wasn't her whom he was interested in.

The next day, he called me into his office. Everything happened so fast. All of sudden, his hands were under my dress, touching my thighs and bum, and his lips were kissing my neck and making their way down my body. I didn't know what to do, so I just ran away from him and his office; I was lucky to get away. After that, I didn't know what to do. I remember sitting in the shower the next morning and just crying. I knew I couldn't tell my mother because I knew she would never believe he found me attractive over her. He was a very well-respected man in our small town, so I knew I couldn't go to the police. I knew that no one would believe me. What's more, if I was to have any chance of getting into that university, I had to graduate from this school—and his gymnasium—normally. I couldn't change my school in the last year of my time there. But it was still eight more long months until graduation. That's a long time to avoid a man intent on raping you. The only person I told about this was my friend. She was the only shoulder I had to cry on.

I also knew I was in trouble, so I told my mother that the university in the city nearest to us was fine with me instead. Somehow—I'm not sure how—the whole situation got resolved. He didn't stop trying to be alone with me, but I managed to dodge his attempts to rape me. I fear many other girls in my school were not so lucky, but I was not among them. I told my mother 20 years after it had happened, and you know what? She didn't believe me. She couldn't believe that someone would choose me over her.

This was the reality of my adolescence. If we look back at Erikson's stages of psychosocial development, we can see that during this time of my life, I was developing my identity. Failure to develop an integrated identity results in role confusion, and with a constantly critical mother, an ailing, distant father figure, and a lack of acceptance among my peers, the addition of a traumatic event like an attempted rape only further complicated the situation. You can understand how this would make me question my self-worth and cause difficulties in accepting myself for who I am. In fact, I didn't really know who I was or what my purpose in life would be. **How about you? Can you identify a stage where you might have not experienced the ideal outcome?** To really understand how this kind of dysfunctional family environment can affect personality structure and organization, we have to delve a little deeper into transactional analysis and personality organization.

Understanding the Levels of Personality Organization

Otto Kernberg was an Austrian-American psychoanalyst who identified several levels of personality organization. These are the following:

- Psychotic Personality Organization
- Borderline Personality Organization
- Neurotic Personality Organization
- Mature Personality Organization

Kernberg wanted to identify how personality organization progresses to better understand personality disorders. He wanted to understand how our psyche develops. He based his categories on the types and use of psychological defense mechanisms, the extent to which an individual is able to perceive reality, one's identity integration, awareness and control of aggression, and to what extent they are guided by moral ideals and values. Initially, we all start out with primitive defense mechanisms, like projecting our unflattering qualities onto other people. We don't use more mature defense mechanisms, like rationalization. Likewise, we are prone to "magical thinking:" we are initially unable to differentiate self from non-self, control our aggression, or really have a moral code. As we grow and learn from our parents and society, we progress from these primitive mechanisms of defense; we increasingly learn to cast aside our magical thinking, adopt morals, and learn who we are. We move into the borderline spectrum within about two years in response to our early life circumstances. Between three to six years old is when most people move into the neurotic level of personality organization. This is when children learn about guilt and shame. Typically, we reach the mature level at approximately 25 years old. This is how our personality organizes; however, trauma in the form of abuse or neglect can stifle that progression. When that happens, a person may be stuck at a so-called more primitive level of personality organization; with severe trauma, they can even regress to a previous level. Let's explore each level to better understand the characteristics of each and how that level can affect our behavior.

Psychotic Personality Organization

This is where we all start as infants. This is the least healthy level of personality organization, and it includes people with severely disorganized personalities. People in this category have poorly compromised reality testing, meaning they may hear or see things that are not present, or they may believe they have special powers or are receiving special messages. They also have an inconsistent sense of self and others, and they use extremely immature defense mechanisms when stressed. These individuals don't have a concept of themselves as distinct from other people. Therefore, they have difficulty determining experiences and perceptions that come from their own mind as opposed to others or their environment. They can't cope well at all with stress, and they don't function well in society. Although some of this thinking may be normal in an infant, it becomes pathological in older individuals.

Borderline Personality Organization

You may have heard of Borderline Personality Disorder, and although this level of personality organization includes people with BPD, they are not the same thing. In this level, reality testing is mostly intact, but they have a fragmented sense of self and others. In a normal progression, this typically occurs in response to life experiences encountered during the first two years of life. But with trauma, a person can get stuck at this level. Their sense of self remains fragmented. That means they don't have a consistent view of themselves or others across situations and over time. For example, emotionally mature people can be angry at someone but still identify that person as good and love them. People with a fragmented self identity and inability to recognize others' have difficulty maintaining positive feelings about people when they're angry at them. This is because, in part, they tend to see people as extensions of their own identity. They can't see people as mixtures of bad and good; instead, they think in binary terms: you're either all good or all bad. This is known as splitting, and it's a common primitive defense mechanism employed by people with this kind of personality organization. As you might imagine, this can create numerous repetitive problems in their interpersonal relationships. All of this translates into recurring issues, which can involve problems like substance abuse, obesity, dependence, and toxic partners.

Neurotic Personality Organization

These individuals are similar to those with a mature personality organization, in that they have intact reality testing, a good sense of self and others, and a fairly good understanding of what their life goals are. Most people move into this level between three and six years of age, when they first encounter feelings like guilt or shame. This is the beginning of recognizing that there are consequences for one's actions. From here, healthy individuals continue to mature. Those who don't get stuck at an earlier level usually have a more consistent direction and understanding of their purpose. They are able to form strong, committed relationships and can view other people more accurately. They are mostly successful at coping with stress effectively, but they tend to use neurotic defense mechanisms like repression to deal with stressful situations. This is the main difference between this personality organization and that of a mature personality organization. They have a secure attachment style, but they may not have experienced success at every level of Erikson's human psychosocial development.

Mature Personality Organization

This is the healthiest level of personality organization, and in a normal progression, individuals reach this level by approximately 25 years of age. People with mature personality organizations have more reliable defense mechanisms when things go wrong. These include using humor to process stressful situations. They may also use something like anticipation to work out the logical consequences of various behaviors. People with this type of personality organization also have a well-integrated sense of self, as well as healthy representations of "other." They additionally have good reality testing capabilities. Basically, this person is well-adjusted with respect to their identity and the world around them. They would also have a secure attachment style and would have experienced the ideal outcomes associated with each stage of psychosocial development.

In general, the mature and neurotic levels of personality organization are at the healthier end of the spectrum, whereas the borderline and psychotic levels are at the more disordered end of the spectrum. Those with borderline and psychotic personality organizations would have insecure attachment styles, and they would have failed to achieve optimal outcomes in several stages of psychosocial development. They have a fragmented recognition of their identity and think in polarized patterns of all good or all bad. They often change careers, romantic partners, and life goals very rapidly and haphazardly; this is an incredibly painful way to live.

So Where Does Codependency Fit Into the Picture?

Everyone is dependent to some degree, and everyone needs a little help from their friends and family from time to time. But sometimes, that need can become excessive to the degree that the dependent person becomes clingy or *craves* that connection with other people. They may become submissive in an attempt to get their needs met, and they may even humiliate themselves in that regard. However, dependency is not just an individual state; all cultures encourage some level of dependency. Some within a culture may be denied their personal autonomy. For example, the very young, the very old, sick people, and criminals are all people whom our culture, and virtually every other culture, will make legally dependent on some authority. It's only when such dependency doesn't conform to sociocultural norms that it becomes pathological. Codependency is a condition that shares many overlapping symptoms with Dependent Personality Disorder (DPD). The distinction between the two is found in the nature of the dependent relationship. Codependents focus their dependency traits on a specific person, whereas people with DPD display dependent traits toward others in general. The difference is really of degree rather than kind.

Codependency is when someone becomes highly dependent on someone in their life. Their dependence is so complete that their self-esteem and identity are negatively affected, and they identify themselves *with* that dependency. They are constantly preoccupied with over-the-top worries, and their fear of abandonment paralyzes them. This turmoil makes them indecisive, and even simple decisions end up beyond their capacity. For that reason, they usually won't initiate projects or events on their own. Their fears, coupled with indecisiveness, cause them to seek reassurance repeatedly from everyone around them. In essence, they are handing over responsibility for their own life to other people. They don't trust themselves to be responsible for their own happiness. They have delegated that responsibility to other people in their lives. Then, by dedicating themselves to ensuring others are happy and satisfied, they can then find their own happiness through them. In short, codependents love themselves by loving someone else so intensely that they give themselves over to that person.

Another quality that codependents lack is an inner compass. They can't realistically assess their own positive qualities, and because they have limited their life by dedicating it to someone else. Those limitations force them to be reliant on input from elsewhere. That causes them to be fearful of losing the support they get from those outside sources. They can't disagree with or criticize them since they are reliant on their support. Consequently, they cater to the needs of the people to whom they have dedicated themselves. They were taught to behave this way as a child. Their parents taught them only to expect conditional, transactional love. If they behave well and provide what their parents want from them, they will be rewarded with their love. This unjust treatment can cause a rage in the child, and they then may either direct that rage inwardly, producing a masochist or a depressive illness, or outwardly, resulting in psychopathy. Like their rage, their love can be directed inwardly, contributing to narcissism, or outwardly, contributing to codependence.

In the case of codependence, the individual who suffers from this seeks to merge with their love object. In that way, they can love themselves by providing love to the object of their affection. This dependence becomes the affected individual's comfort zone—their best friend in a way. The individual who exhibits codependency is both fixated on and reliant upon their state of dependence. It's a difficult trap to extract oneself from because it disguises itself as love. You tell yourself that you're only doing what you're doing because it's a demonstration of your love. The problem is that you don't truly love yourself, and you're trying to fill that void by pouring your love into someone else. The need is so strong that you start to believe you can't live without your dependence, which you see incarnate in the person to whom you're addicted. It's a dysfunctional pattern of behavior in relationships; it's learned, and it's something a child witnesses in parental interactions. Fortunately, the positive aspect behind all this is that it is acquired knowledge, and therefore, this behavior can be unlearned.

The Realization of My Codependence

After I left for university, I came upon some very difficult times. I had to survive all alone in a big city, and sometimes, I didn't even have enough money for dinner. I would have to walk home from university because I didn't have the money to pay for transportation. Still, I felt happy; I thought I was doing okay. I was away from my mother's harsh criticism and the difficulties of life at home. I felt happy inside without all of the fighting and complaining. I survived those lean times, graduated with my degree, and ended up young and successful. I had opened my own little business, had a car and an apartment, and did my best to take care of my mother by buying her new clothes and sending her on vacation every year. I thought it would make her proud of me.

My father died right after I graduated. I organized his funeral, but I couldn't stop blaming him for getting sick. I kept thinking that if he had stayed healthy, I wouldn't have had to suffer the hardships I did while in school. I also thought he could have protected me from the troubles I had in my young life.

At that time, I was not choosing my relationships; the men in my life were choosing me because of my looks and success. As you can see by how I was still devoted to taking care of my mother and blaming my father for my problems, I was fully codependent at that time. The years of my mother's harsh criticism and my father's neglect had taught me that love was conditioned on my performance. I had also been taking care of someone from a very early age—first my brother, then my mother and father. I had turned that love outward and invested it in external sources of validation. I needed to pour my love into someone so I could then love myself vicariously. I jumped from one codependent relationship to another in my romantic partners. By 33, I was divorced for a second time. I had married a narcissist—a familiar kind of relationship—and I was left feeling completely empty and horribly depressed. If you would like to read more about this turning point in my life, I have written another book on the topic: *My Toxic Husband: Loving and Breaking Up with a Narcissistic Man—Start Your Psychopath-free Life Now!* This experience was when I started to realize that there was something wrong with me. I couldn't see it because, remember, it's easy to convince ourselves that our codependency is just an expression of our loving nature. But I knew that I couldn't seem to have a normal relationship, and without that, I would never have the family I had always dreamed of having. I had to analyze the reasons behind my poor decision-making processes and find ways to modify them. And so, I started psychotherapy.

Exercise #3

Your Codependence

Codependency is not a distinct personality disorder recognized by the DSM-5, but it shares many overlapping symptoms with Dependent Personality Disorder.

Reflect on the following diagnostic criteria for DPD and on whether they are true for you. Although this is not a true diagnosis, it can help you determine your patterns of behavior:

- All-consuming, unrealistic fear of being abandoned.
- Anxiety or feelings of helplessness when alone.
- Inability to manage life responsibilities without seeking help from others.
- Problems stating an opinion out of fear of losing support or approval.

- Strong drive to get support from others, even choosing to do unenjoyable things to get it.
- Trouble making everyday decisions without input or reassurance from others.
- Trouble starting or completing projects due to a lack of self-confidence or ability to make decisions.
- Urge to seek a new relationship for support and approval when a close relationship ends.

If you have checked yes to five or more of these criteria, and if you focus your dependency traits on one person rather than everyone in general, you're likely codependent. Now, think about some of the symptoms of codependency, such as avoiding personal responsibility, difficulty being alone, being overly sensitive to criticism, lacking self-confidence, and having difficulty with everyday decisions. Contemplate your early years to identify the root cause of these symptoms. Try to think of the first time you felt any of them. For example, when was the first time you felt fearful of being alone? When was the first time you believed you couldn't make a simple decision without input from someone else? Attempt to recollect instances from your childhood where you believed you lacked the ability to perform tasks independently or that you were insufficient. This might have been because of a critical parent—as was my case—or it may have come from an offhand comment made by someone you admire. Whatever the situation, write down your thoughts and feelings about that memory in your journal. Writing it down will help you recognize the origins of your problem. This is where we begin. We must understand the nature of the problem before we can seek treatment for it. Rage on the page to release some of that pent-up negative emotion that helped form your dependency. Then, take five deep breaths, and let yourself know that you love yourself, and it's time to begin that healing journey.

Chapter 4

The Signs of Relationship Addiction

I discovered through my own healing journey that an overriding core belief I had adopted about myself was that I was not enough. I had learned my place in childhood and had been told that I was nothing special. I was not ugly, nor beautiful. I was not stupid, nor smart. I was plain, average, and nothing to write home about. When other people would tell me I was beautiful, I just thought they were being polite. Even after all the years of therapy, my education in the field of psychology, and my practice as a psychotherapist, I still sometimes struggle with my internal support mechanisms and confidence. Every time I believe I've overcome my past, I hear my mother accusing or devaluing me. Although I no longer consciously accept those negative statements, her abuse was something that I incorporated as part of my core identity. It's something often referred to as introjection, and for many, it typically occurs in the first three years of life.

Introjection and the Mother-Child Relationship

Introjection is the opposite of projection. Projection is when someone else projects their own feelings or characteristics onto another person. Introjection, however, happens when you internalize the beliefs, emotions, attitudes, etc., of other people. It's very common between children and their parents—particularly their mother—and although it occurs throughout your development, it is most pronounced between the ages of three and six years of age, when a child wants to be an adult, and of course, they want to be like their mother or father. When you introject, you identify with another person so strongly that you can't separate yourself from them. What's even more insidious is that introjection happens without a lot of thought. In fact, it can happen without any thought whatsoever. When a newborn infant sees the face of a loving, supportive, and comforting mother, they introject those attitudes, and that stays with them throughout their life. If, on the other hand, a newborn infant is met with a mother's face that is irritated, neglectful, and projecting negative emotions and thoughts, that infant introjects those attitudes. The infant isn't analyzing them; they are simply accepting them as part of their reality and part of their identity.

Introjections are also not something you can access consciously. These are attitudes you've adopted and accepted as true. You don't have a distinct memory of being told something or something happening to you. You just have a vague feeling of either positivity or negativity. For those with positive experiences of introjection, you adopt certain traits such as compassion, loyalty, and morality. Of course, these can be very helpful during difficult times. You don't consciously think about them; you simply feel them pervasively and intensely. To give you an example, if you introjected positive traits from your mother as an infant, and someone tells you that you're "just like your mother," you would experience happy, vivid, and warm feelings and memories. It's almost like she's a spirit inside your head emanating love for you.

If, on the other hand, you introjected negative traits or emotions from your mother as an infant, you may feel a pervasive sense of worthlessness. You can't put your finger on exactly why that would be, but you feel incompetent, guilty, or inept. You may also find it difficult to readily discover and form a strong identity. As you grow older, you start to lack self-confidence, and you also develop a negative internal voice or dialogue. You become your unloving, critical mother. She's like a scary ghost living in your head, filling you with self-doubt and low self-worth. What's even worse is that you won't know that it came from her. One client realized she had introjected her mother's outright contempt for her as an infant. It left her believing that not only was she not enough, but she was also undeserving of anything good. She related a story about a computer she recently bought that wasn't working well. It was brand new, and still, it wasn't working as it should. That's frustrating in general, but for her, it was devastating, and she couldn't quite put her finger on why. When she analyzed it further, she realized that she had introjected her mother's negative feelings toward her to the extent that she had a pervasive belief that nothing would ever work out for her, even something as simple as a computer working normally. Does this story resonate with you at all? Think about what your pervasive beliefs are. You usually encounter them when you're frustrated like that client.

You can similarly introject negative or positive traits from your father. I had a client who had introjected her father's assessment of her as a "real shit." She carried that image of herself inside for many years without fully realizing how it got there. It was like a secret name she had given herself, but it really came from her father. Although you might surpass the criticism you remember receiving from your parents, you may be unable to shake the feeling of inadequacy that you internalized during infancy. This is what happened to me. When I was old enough to remember my mother's critical statements, I had already introjected that worthlessness, to where her criticisms only seemed like valid justification for what I already felt inside.

Though I no longer accept my mother's criticisms and devaluation, the dark shadow of introjection still haunts me. That's why I hear her voice in my head telling me I'm worthless, wrong, and undeserving of happiness. That's why it took me almost 40 years to clean out the wounds of the trauma she inflicted on me my entire life. It's the trauma of rejection—something reflected even in her recent remarks, where she asked me how my current husband could bear to live with me. She also told me that she couldn't understand what he saw in me; this isn't the first time she's said this kind of thing about a man in my life.

While I used to take those criticisms to heart, I now at least recognize them for the abuse they are. This is part of what created my need to please others in order to love myself. I tried for so many years to pour my love into my mother, so I could feel loved vicariously through her. I wanted her acceptance and love. I wanted her to see me and think that I was special, at least to her. That never happened, but it left a dark legacy: my codependency. Let us delve deeper into the various categories of codependency to gain a better understanding.

Codependent Types

Codependency is a complex problem. It is a multi-faceted defense mechanism designed to protect the codependent from their own fears and needs. They've been taught that they don't matter except as related to how they can care for others. But that manifests in different ways that are related to specific etiologies of the problem. There are five categories of codependence. Let's take a closer look at each one.

- ❖ **Codependency Designed to Alleviate Fear of Abandonment**

Codependency that develops to alleviate fears of abandonment produces people who are clingy, smothering, and often panic. They exhibit self-negating submissiveness in the hope that they can prevent their loved ones from leaving them. They also don't want to attain any level of true autonomy or independence. They merge with their loved ones, and if they perceive signs of abandonment, whether real or imagined, they see that as a kind of self-annihilation. It is literally as if they are abandoning themselves or as if a part of them is dying. As a result, they are not above using emotional blackmail and threats to force their victims to comply with what they want.

❖ Codependency to Cope with a Fear of Losing Control

This type of codependent feigns helplessness to get those around them to cater to their needs and desires. They appear as drama queens, and their lives are of almost constant instability and chaos. These individuals never grow up, and they utilize self-imputed deficiencies and disabilities as weapons to force their loved ones to treat them as emotional and/or physical invalids. They will also use blackmail and threats to force compliance with their wishes.

❖ Vicarious Codependents

Just as you might imagine, these are codependents who live vicariously through others. They live in the shadow of their targets and bask in the glow of their reflected glory. They see themselves as the "woman behind the man" or the "man behind the woman." They imagine that it's really their support and love that allows their target to thrive. As the song goes, they see themselves as "the wind beneath the wings" of their target. They suspend their lives and desires in favor of supporting those of their loved one, and they see that sacrifice as their greatest accomplishment.

❖ Oscillating Codependents

This codependent is often also called a codependent or borderline narcissist. They oscillate between periods when they exhibit codependent behaviors, like being extremely clingy, and periods when they are more aloof, detached, and neglectful. When they're exhibiting codependent behaviors, they interpret those as intimacy, and when they're aloof, they view themselves as reclaiming their personal space. They will also sometimes form a shared psychosis with their intimate partners. This is something known as *folie à deux*, and in its extreme form, it's been seen in cases of pairs of serial killers, such as the Hillside Stranglers and Leonard Lake and Charles Ng.

In milder cases, it usually manifests as a loss of autonomy for both partners. The reason behind it is the all-consuming fear of abandonment. That's also true for the aloof oscillation. The idea behind this is that the codependent individual is quitting before they get fired. They abandon their intimate partner to preserve an illusion of control over the situation. Another common feature of this codependency type is something known as coextensivity. This is where codependent individuals expect their partners to read their minds. They believe their intimacy should allow them to intuit each other's thoughts, emotions, and moods. This type of codependent will also use shifting boundaries to create dependence in their partner. They become behaviorally unpredictable to confuse their partners and keep them guessing.

❖ Counterdependents

The last category is one that has only been identified recently. It's that of counterdependents. These are individuals who despise authority and will clash with authority figures, such as their parents, boss, and the police. It's in these acts of defiance that this type of codependent derives their self-identity. They are uncompromisingly independent, but they are also controlling, self-centered, and even aggressive. They force other people to affirm their view of the world and expectations. Because of their fiercely independent nature, they are extremely fearful of intimacy, which makes them feel as though they are being held captive. This causes them to be bad team players. They consider themselves to be lone wolves, yet they engage in approach-avoidance repetition compulsion cycles. This is where they are hesitant to approach others and become engaged in close relationships. That is followed by a fear and avoidance of any level of commitment. This type of codependent doesn't just fear their own weaknesses; they actually dread them. They may compensate for that by projecting an image of being omnipotent, omniscient, or superior. That might sound like narcissism to you—and in fact, most overt or grandiose narcissists are counterdependent. They have buried their emotions and needs under layers of scar tissue that formed as a result of the abuse they endured as a child. They use their grandiosity as a shield against their insecurity, shame, and self-loathing.

Situational Codependence

It is also possible that some may develop codependent behaviors in the wake of a life crisis. Many who go through a divorce or some other form of abandonment may begin to exhibit codependent behaviors. When this happens, the person usually experiences a complex set of emotions, the role of which is to resolve the inner turmoil they are experiencing as a result of undesirable codependent behaviors. For example, someone may be dumped by their romantic partner, and initially, they may feel liberated. But the abandonment leaves them feeling lonesome and somewhat disoriented subconsciously. This can cause them to rush into a new relationship before fully grieving the old one and without fully vetting the new one. On some level, the person has always dreaded being lonely, but with no real solution to being abandoned so suddenly, the individual suppresses these feelings and is unable to cope with them. When left alone, that suppressed dread reemerges, and it causes the person to engage in codependent behaviors to avoid being left alone ever again. The codependence, in this case, is a dysfunctional defense mechanism designed to fend off abandonment.

Because this kind of person often has a balanced and strong sense of self, they are unhappy with their codependent behavior because they have always seen themselves as strong and confident with a well-regulated sense of self-worth. This new part of their behavior is frustrating—it runs counter to their self-image, and they dedicate themselves to getting rid of these unbecoming behaviors. To get rid of them, the person subconsciously chooses someone who is not right for them, then goes about proving to themselves that this person is wrong for them before discarding that person. By taking control of the situation, they are reestablishing their autonomy, and they can then be assured that they are rid of their codependency.

Situational codependency can be characterized by a suppressed, underlying fear of abandonment. It hides until awakened by some life crisis, such as a divorce, an empty nest, or the death of a loved one. At first, the individual may feel exhilarated with their new-found freedom, but that doesn't last, and it actually may enhance their anxiety. The person might even worry about their finding this freedom intoxicating and choose to remain alone for the rest of their life. They are also plagued by nagging fears that they need to find someone quickly; they're not getting any younger, after all. They develop situational codependence to cope with the internal turmoil it causes. As a result, they quickly attract an intimate partner to forestall their abandonment. But most situational codependents tend to be ego-dystonic. That means they look inward to determine the problem and examine their dissatisfaction. Because their codependence is so contrary to their true nature, they reestablish their autonomy by getting rid of the new partner. The person may not be aware of these internal dynamics.

My Type of Codependence

My mother was the product of her upbringing, generation, and environment, as is true of anyone. She was subjected to her own trauma, which caused her to develop in very narcissistic ways unconsciously. As a result, she created a dysfunctional family environment that was chaotic and unsupportive as an adult. She was jealous of her daughter—as is true of any narcissistic mother—and she made her son into a golden child, which is also typical. Because of her jealousy, she constantly devalued and blamed me for anything that went wrong, but in her mind, she was making me stronger. Although she may have been doing the best she could, given her own trauma, she also had unrealistic expectations for me and parentified me at a young age. Like most children in that kind of dysfunctional family environment, I always assumed the problem was me. And my mother manipulated me to ensure I believed that for her own reasons. I learned that love was conditional and dependent upon my good behavior, a goal that shifted constantly. My mother was seeking to undermine my self-esteem, self-confidence, and self-worth, perhaps because she believed I might otherwise become too vain. I desired her approval, and so I continued to give in the futile hope that someday, she would see, accept, and love me. Her approval became my source of self-esteem. Her blame-shifting caused me to feel guilty and somehow responsible for things that were clearly beyond my control. Because I felt responsible and couldn't seem to do anything correctly, I felt worthless; I was not enough. It's important to understand that I'm not blaming her, *per se*, for I do believe that what happened has made me a better person. By understanding the legacy of intergenerational trauma, we can finally break the cycle. It's not about hating or blaming a parent for your problems; it's about understanding their origins so you can grow into the best possible version of yourself.

As a child, I lacked the cognitive abilities and life experience to understand that how my mother treated me wasn't healthy. I just thought that this was the way everyone's mother acted. Every child thinks that way about their family. Your family is the norm in your mind because it's all you know. Because my self-worth was firmly rooted in my mother's approval, my coping strategy became one of trying to please her. That became a pattern that followed me into adulthood. I sought intimate, familiar partners because they treated me like my mother had. I continued to try to please them to feel loved. I was trying to love myself by pouring my devotion into my partner and basking in the glow of their gratitude. Because I was picking dysfunctional partners, however, there never was any gratitude—just like there never was any gratitude from my mother. I was a vicarious codependent looking for love in all the wrong places. I was looking for love through my relationships with other people. But my fear of rejection also created elements of oscillating codependency. I would often invent a reason to break off a relationship so I could avoid the pain of rejection later on. The problem, however, was with my relationship with myself. This illustrates the complexity of codependency; no one fits into a single, neat category. There are often overlapping elements in codependent types.

It's only been within the last couple of years that I closely examined why my mother treated me the way she did. I can sometimes see something that looks like love for me in her eyes, but it never shows in how she treats me. That's because to show her love would make her vulnerable, and as a narcissist, she couldn't let herself do that. I used to be angry about this, but now I'm just sorry. I'm sorry for her and her mental condition. I'm sorry for the child I was who never got the love she deserved. I'm sorry that I spent so much time in my life blaming myself for something that was not my fault. I'm sorry that it took me so long to figure out that I deserved love just for being me. I'm sorry for these things, but I'm grateful too. I'm grateful that I was able to discover why I now engage in these patterns of behavior. I'm grateful that I have found my true self-worth. I'm grateful for the gifts my childhood gave me. It was hard, but I survived, and I survived because I am resilient. I'm grateful that I have found new, healthier coping strategies for dealing with life's challenges, those challenges also including toxic people. I'm grateful that I am now giving myself the unconditional love that my mother should have given me. In this way, my criticizing, distant mother gave me the power I needed to fight for the best life I could have and prove that I could not only heal, but also thrive. My pain created my power, and this is true of any traumatizing event. It's a cliche, but what doesn't kill you truly does make you stronger if you search for that which suffering has brought to you. Think about your own situation and how the problems you've faced in life have made you stronger. What did you learn from them, and how have you used that to prove to your parents or the world that you can rise above it to find success and happiness? How did you make lemonade out of the lemons life gave you?

My mother may never be able to see me as a unique individual separate from her own identity; she may never be able to love me for who I am, and while I still hope for that unconditional love from her, I can now see her through compassionate eyes. The mind of a narcissist is filled with fear. They have to be hypervigilant and in control of every situation they encounter. That's an impossible task, and it must be a torturous existence inside her mind. But I can no longer live in the hope that somehow, someday, she will change. I have to move on with my life. I have to let go of the past.

While this is something that happened to me, it is no longer "my story." I have a new story—one of healing and self-love. I have my mother figure secure inside of me. I have evicted the introjected mother figure I had for most of my life and replaced her with my own image of unconditional love; my inner mother is giving unconditional love to my inner child. She is helping that little me to heal. Even my mother sees the change in me, and of course, she doesn't like it. But that's okay because I do. Each person has their own story and their own life puzzle, and each of us has to complete the puzzle for ourselves. We can't do it for anyone else, and no one can do it for us. We must walk our own path. I continue on my path of healing, but what does your path look like? What is your story, and how did you get to this point?

Exercise #4

What's Your Type?

To assess your type of codependency, you'll need to consider your answers to the following questions carefully. Be honest, and remember—you're doing this to help yourself be free from your fears.

- When your intimate partner leaves for work or to go out with friends, do you feel anxious?
- Do you ever say something to a loved one in an effort to get them to respond to you in a particular way? For example, you might say something like, "I'm so stupid," to get them to disagree with you.
- Do you secretly wish that other people would recognize your efforts in supporting someone you love?
- Do you consider yourself independent?
- Have you ever feigned an illness to get a loved one to stay at home with you?
- Have you ever threatened suicide if a loved one leaves you?
- Do you like to think of yourself as a rebel?
- Do you see yourself as the star of a Greek tragedy?
- Do you think the reason your loved one is successful is because of your support?
- Do you ever feel like you push people away and then pull them close again?

Once you've answered these questions, reflect on your answers and determine which types of codependency they fit the best. There can be overlaps, as exemplified by my own story, but there is likely one that will fit better than the others. Remember, the goal is to understand the nature of your type of codependency fully. That knowledge will pave the way toward your personal healing path.

Chapter 5

Your Restless Inner Child

Do you remember when you were a child and the summers seemed endless? Do you remember being fascinated by the simple beauty of a butterfly? Do you remember the wonder of discovery when first learning about the world around you? What about just laying on a hillside and watching the clouds go by? The joy of playing with your friends, the laughter, and the freedom you felt as you just enjoyed life?

The peace, wonder, curiosity, playfulness, and joy of just being—those are the gifts a child possesses. A child is like a budding scientist exploring the world around them and taking in new knowledge and experiences. They observe, experiment, and learn. They are unencumbered by preconceived notions of what should and shouldn't be. They accept what is, and they adapt. But there's a dark side to that as well: when there is abuse, neglect, indifference, or perhaps even just distance in the family, children absorb those experiences, and it can affect them for the rest of their lives. We have learned that even before an infant is able to speak or walk, they are already absorbing the experiences from their environment and caretakers.

That inner child that's a part of each one of us remembers those experiences and holds onto anything traumatic. Specifically, they hold our memories, emotions, and beliefs from the past, and they also store our hopes and dreams for the future. They remember how grandma smelled when she hugged you and the look of pride on your mother or father's face when you mastered something. They remember what we desired to be when we grew up. They remember that feeling of awe and wonder you got when you envisioned doing what you loved so much.

Your inner child also, however, remembers what it felt like to be bullied at school. They remember how you felt when your teacher scoffed at your awkward answer to a seemingly easy question. They also remember if your mother or father didn't look at you as an infant with love; if instead, they looked at you with irritation or outright disdain. Basically, your inner child has been inside of you, storing away any memories, feelings, and thoughts you experienced when those events happened. Your inner child is like a vast storehouse of sensations, good and bad, that you've had every moment of your life. Even long after you've forgotten an incident, your inner child remembers the incident and your accompanying emotions. That little part of you is with you even today, waiting to be heard, understood, and loved. They are always communicating with you, but you may not know how to listen and respond.

That's the goal of focusing on your inner child—to see, acknowledge, and embrace them with the unconditional love they deserve. It's important to do that because your inner child can affect your life significantly. You might experience their influence when you're starting a new intimate relationship, and as soon as that person starts to get close to you, you are seized by an uncontrollable sense of fear. Your inner child is letting you know there's a problem that you need to address. They are crying out for attention because they remember an experience from your past. Ignoring them won't do because they can make or break your happiness. If you're feeling frustrated in some part of your life, that's likely your inner child trying to get your attention. Tending to them is one of the most important things you will do in your life.

The Origins of Inner Child Theory

Eric Berne first introduced the term "Inner Child" in the 60s. He associated it with the child ego state, which he described as having become enriched to become the "Inner Child." Later, researchers began exploring how a patient can reclaim their inner child to rediscover their deeper selves and heal old wounds. It became a way to nurture one's psychological well-being when examining trauma related to codependency. Inner child healing workshops became a way for traumatized individuals to do this work in a safe group setting. These workshops allow them to connect with their inner child, soothe their wounds, and then experience a rebirth into a new caretaking experience, where they would learn how to parent their inner child with love and support. Essentially, you would give them what they should have gotten from your caretakers, but that didn't happen. After all, we are all adult kids just trying to understand our world.

Studies consistently show that people of all ages can benefit from this type of intervention. It can help heal old wounds, and doing so can then work to help you become more childlike in beneficial ways. Healthy children have an undeniable capacity for finding the good in every situation, and they are infinitely creative. That's what I mean when I say healing your inner child will help you reclaim that childlike innocence beneficially. You become your own hero, and you save yourself from the inner demons that seek to undermine you. You can overcome old fears and anxieties that are making you feel stuck. When you heal those old wounds, you can see and change the unhelpful behavioral patterns that are preventing you from blossoming.

How Do You Connect to and Heal Your Inner Child?

There are two steps to cultivating a relationship with your inner child. You must first make that connection to begin a dialogue and develop a relationship with them. You have to see them and be willing to listen to them. After making that connection, the next step is to listen to what they're telling you. You have to learn about what scares them, hurts them, what they dream about, and what their hopes are. Once you know that, you can then provide your inner child with what they need to thrive. By giving them what they need, you are giving *yourself* what you need. What you do for your inner child, you do for yourself.

Connecting with Your Inner Child

To connect with your inner child, you have to connect with your core beliefs. One of the best ways to do that is through meditation. When you sit in silence with the emotions that have been triggered by an event, you can begin exploring what is actually causing your reaction. For example, one of the things that used to trigger me was criticism. Because of my mother's constant criticism, my inner child was hypersensitive to anything critical that anyone would say to me. When I began doing inner child work, I would call up a recent incident where I had been triggered by some kind of criticism. I would meditate on the incident so I could experience the feeling again. Afterwards, I would go a little deeper and explore the first time I felt that way. Inevitably, I would see a little girl being criticized in some similar way by her angry mother. I would see that little me shrinking in shame. When I was a child, I tried so hard to please my mother, but no matter what I did, she had some kind of criticism. It generated a core belief of shame and unworthiness in that little me. When I tapped into those emotions, I could see myself withering under her critical assessment of not just my actions that she had issues with, but of who I was. When I could see that little girl being crushed by the shame her mother was instilling in her, I was then able to comfort, tell her that there is nothing wrong with her, and assure her that I would always be here to take care of her. I could address that pain and help her heal that old wound.

Healing Your Inner Child

Just by shining a light on that trauma, we can achieve a lot of healing. When we listen to our inner child, we give ourselves a way to process that old pain. Often, the trauma that you receive at a young age gets "stuck" in your body. We were never able to process it, and for that reason, it stayed stuck. It is that trapped trauma that continues to affect our daily lives negatively. Your inner child needs to be heard and understood, and they need your attention. Sometimes they just need your support, but in other cases, they can also give you guidance. My little girl didn't have a voice all those years ago; she couldn't speak up to defend herself. When she sees that I'm in a similar situation as an adult, she gets distressed because she wants me to speak up not just for myself, but for her as well. She needs me to take care of myself and, thereby, take care of her. She is insistent on that, and to make her point, she is able to generate all kinds of uncomfortable feelings that would affect my relationships. Once I start doing that, once I start meeting her needs – which are also my needs – the uncomfortable feelings go away. Think about this in terms of your own relationships. What is your inner child saying to you, and when do they speak up?

When Your Inner Child is Happy

When your inner child is happy and healthy, it will fill you with energy and creativity. Gone are the latent feelings of shame and fear. Failure is something that happens to you occasionally; it is not who you are. You no longer need to act out impulsively, and you don't need approval from others. You can blossom into who you've always believed you were because you are anchored by a strong, healthy, internal "family." Gone are the insecurity and introjected negative mother figure. You replace her as a healthy parental figure for your inner child. You feel confident, rooted, secure, and comfortable in your own skin, and you can see the path that is right for you more clearly. Additionally, your inner child can act as a kind of guide. They are more open to you now that you're meeting their needs, and they can alert you to your deepest emotions and desires, while also helping you take better care of yourself. We often don't know when our subconscious is trying to tell us something, but when we're in communication with our inner child, we have a direct line to those fears and desires. This can help us uncover the hidden emotions we may have buried long ago. It's a deeply satisfying form of healing.

What are the Symptoms of a Restless Inner Child?

So how can you know if your inner child is trying to get your attention? What are the symptoms that suggest you need to do this kind of work? Here are some of the more common indications that your inner child likely needs your attention.

- Feelings of shame, guilt, and/or pain.
- You're a workaholic, and you feel you need to achieve or produce to get approval or to feel as though you belong.
- You are always thinking about the past or future. You are never in the present.
- You regularly feel anxious and fearful.
- You are rigid in your behavior and personality, and you believe you must be perfect. Failure on any level distresses you greatly.

- You have difficulty celebrating victories in life and accepting compliments. You readily accept criticism but feel that any compliment is just someone "being nice."
- You have a pattern of unhealthy relationships, or you avoid committed relationships altogether.
- You sabotage yourself in your relationships and career path. You often do this through addictive behaviors.
- You are an underachiever. You have great potential, but you just don't do the work.
- You have a negative internal critic. You ruminate on what you have said in conversations, sometimes for days after the conversation has taken place.

These are just a few of the signs that indicate your inner child is restless. For each of these, there is an underlying core belief that you've accepted about yourself.

What are Core Beliefs?

Core beliefs represent the essence of how we see ourselves, the world around us, and other people. They also involve what we think of our potential and what we might do in the future. They are "stored" by our inner child, since they form early in life. Certain situations can activate these core beliefs; for example, I couldn't believe that other people really thought I was attractive. When they would tell me so, I simply thought they were being nice or trying to make me feel better. Why was that? I had adopted a core belief that my mother had told me from an early age that I have nothing to offer anyone—I am ugly and worthless. Because my mother started telling me those things early in life, I simply accepted them. This is what children do, particularly when they're being told by an authority figure that something is true. These core beliefs are deeply rooted and inflexible. They cause you to readily accept any life situation that confirms your core belief and ignore evidence that contradicts it. I couldn't accept a compliment about my appearance, but I could readily accept that my relationships failed because I am inherently worthless.

To challenge these core beliefs, you have to comfort your inner child and show them that they are not true. That means you have to challenge the core beliefs head-on. For example, if you hold a core belief that you're stupid, and that belief is activated because you failed a test in school, you may initially accept that your failure proves that you are stupid. But when you examine it a little more closely and honestly, the truth is that you simply didn't study for the test. You might not have studied because you had to work or you had an emergency come up. You might also be engaging in a form of self-sabotage. All of these are possibilities, but none of them indicate stupidity. Moreover, it wasn't that you couldn't understand the material presented on the test; it was that you were ignorant of the right answer. Ignorance is not the same as stupidity. When you examine the situation objectively, you accumulate evidence to support how your core belief is not true. You can find other examples too, and as they become more apparent, they can be used to convince your inner child that this core belief is not valid. Uncovering your core beliefs is at the heart of inner child work. They represent what your inner child has come to believe, which is a big part of why they can stir up restlessness in your conscious life.

One of my core beliefs was that I was not enough. My mother had reinforced that belief on many occasions, but there's more to that belief than simply what her words told me. I also absorbed it in her face when she looked at me as an infant. She didn't mirror love and acceptance; she mirrored irritation and dissatisfaction. I introjected a message of not being enough for my mother. She loved my brother, and he could do no wrong—he was, after all, the golden child—but I was nothing but a source of disappointment for her from the day I was born until now. This is a strong core belief, and if I'm completely honest, I have yet to banish it forever. But the inner child work I have done has helped me greatly to recognize when that belief gets activated, as well as dealing with it healthier and more effectively. It's important to remember that all of this work is a process. Lifelong trauma is healed over time. The first step is connecting to your inner child and discovering your core beliefs.

Exercise #5

Connection and Discovery

This exercise is designed to help you get in touch with your inner child and discover your core beliefs, and it will provide a template for doing so. You'll need a quiet place for self-reflection and your journal. It can also help to play some meditative music while going through this process.

Connection

- Sit in a quiet place where you won't be disturbed.
- Close your eyes and focus on your breathing.
- Take ten deep breaths that expand your belly and chest.
- When you feel relaxed, call to mind something that happened recently that triggered you—a situation where you had an emotional reaction without fully understanding why.
- Relive the experience and fully feel the emotion it created.
- What emotion are you feeling? Is it shame, anger, pain, or fear? Name it and try to think of the first time you experienced that emotion.
- What is your first conscious memory of feeling that emotion? Who was there? What happened? What was said or done? Why did you feel that emotion? What made you afraid? Who said something that made you feel ashamed? What did they say?

- Look at that little you in that situation. Can you see yourself? Do you see your frightened, ashamed, or angry little self? Can you go up to them and comfort them?
- What is the core belief behind the emotional reaction? What did that little child come to believe because of what someone said or did to them?
- Tell that little you that the core belief they adopted isn't true. Tell them you love them unconditionally and that you will always be there for them.
- Take ten more deep breaths, and when ready, open your eyes.

Reflection

After completing the meditative part of the exercise, write in your journal about what you experienced. Answer the following prompts:

- What was the situation that happened when you first felt that emotion?
- Describe it in detail.
- What did it make you feel?
- What was the core belief you adopted as a result of this interaction?

Write for as long as necessary. Try to get to the root of the belief. For example, you might have felt fear, but what's behind that fear? It may be that you felt afraid because you also felt helpless. The fear only represents one expression of the helplessness you were truly feeling. Then, what kind of core belief did that generate? Did feeling helpless make you adopt the belief that you are weak, inept, and incapable? Did it make you believe you are useless or worthless? As you can see, there may be more complex, underlying beliefs behind your experience. It's important to dig out all the nuances behind your beliefs to truly begin the healing process.

Chapter 6

Gifts from the Shadows

The trauma we experience in life lives on in our shadows, and in that sense, it follows us through life. It has a strong influence on our behavior, and we don't consciously understand why or how it is affecting us. This is what psychologist Carl Jung referred to as "the doorway to the real." It contains our darkest desires, secret shame, and most intense rage. It is formed from our repressed memories and qualities—the parts of us we shun. We learned that these parts of ourselves are unacceptable from our culture or parents. But we can't keep it buried. Like a bizarrely distorted Phoenix, it rises from the ashes of our distant past. It reaches out to force us to acknowledge its presence. And to truly heal from our trauma, we must not only acknowledge its presence, but we must also embrace that darkness. The first part of this process is understanding how the shadow forms and controls our behavior.

How Your Shadow Self Forms

When we're born, we are whole, pure, and untouched by the challenges life brings. That doesn't last long; however, soon after, our shadow is also born. It forms as a byproduct of the interactions we have with our closest family members. These are our caretakers who tend to point out the parts of us that aren't so good. Part of that process is simply our socialization into the culture to which we belong. But often, part of that process involves trauma resulting from unhealthy actions and beliefs of our caretakers. In either case, they teach us to reject those perceived negative parts of ourselves so we can behave appropriately, whether that means within the context of our culture or in our interactions with our family members. Naturally, we learn to repress those parts of ourselves to prevent others from seeing them. After all, we don't want others to see the parts of us that are selfish, aggressive, or shameful in any way. But the shadow doesn't go away. Rather, it rises from the depths of our psyche to radically shape our behavior.

How Does the Shadow Self Affect Our Behavior?

To answer this question, it can help to see a few examples of how the shadow forms and the subsequent effects it has on our lives. Well, look into a few of my clients and friends and see how their shadow selves affected you, even if the intentions behind their caregivers' behavior were good.

One client is an older woman whose mother would always admonish her as a child that "pretty is as pretty does." Her mother was trying to convey that real beauty means being beautiful on the inside. Now, that seems like a pretty good message to teach a child; they need to be more concerned about someone's character than their physical beauty. The client, however, discussed how she distorted this message in a way that a shadow self-formed. She took her mother's saying to heart, to the degree that when she had bad thoughts, she would conclude that she was not pretty on the inside. She was ugly, and that equated to bad. So when she got angry or was selfish or vain, that was proof that she was really ugly. As a result, she repressed her angry, selfish, vain self and would often undermine her best interests in favor of not appearing to be a bad person. She wouldn't express justified anger, for example, or do things that were a necessary part of self-care. It set her up for codependency, in that it often caused her to neglect her needs so she wouldn't appear selfish. Still, on the inside, she sometimes had selfish, angry, and vain thoughts, and thus, she was consumed by shame. This had a dramatic effect on her adult relationships: she became a people pleaser to prove that she was worthy of love and not a bad person.

Another example comes from a male client who was consistently told that he shouldn't cry because "big boys don't cry." This is a common message often passed down from father to son in the attempt to turn boys into men who are acceptably masculine culturally. So as a child, his sensitive side was successfully suppressed and a tough shadow self-formed. When he grew up, he struggled in his relationships because he could not express his emotions, either good or bad, for fear of appearing to be a "sissy." He was also overly aggressive, which brought an end to many of his adult relationships. He became fearful of allowing himself to be seen by his friends and closest family members. He expressed a strong sense of isolation, and as a result, he struggled with loneliness and depression.

What's even worse, the more you repress the shadow, the more it grows and strengthens its influence in your life. As you can see, in the two examples above, the caretakers weren't abusing their children with the messages they sent; they were trying to convey culturally appropriate messages to teach their children how to behave acceptably. They wanted to turn them into what they—and the broader culture—considered *good*. They weren't beating them or emotionally abusing them, but still, the shadow formed as the children interpreted the messages they were receiving. Then, their shadows began to have a strong subconscious effect on their life. Can you think of any examples of this kind of message distortion in your own life? It's not something you can normally see clearly. It often expresses itself as emotions or a ghost-like "sense of what is right." But a distortion of messages is not the only way a shadow can form. Sometimes, the messages are born out of trauma.

How Does Trauma Affect Shadow Formation?

Shadows can also form from different types of trauma, and according to Lise Bourbeau, there are five types of trauma that can interfere with your life:

- Rejection
- Abandonment
- Humiliation
- Betrayal
- Injustice

When exposed to one of these types of trauma, we form a mask as protection against further trauma. When we don that mask, we also repress the part of ourselves that we believe provoked the trauma, which would then become a shadow. I have personally experienced the trauma associated with rejection and abandonment, as well as humiliation. These traumas laid the groundwork for the formation of my codependency. To better understand, let's examine each of these traumas, how they form, and the effects they can have on your life.

1. Rejection

Rejection can happen as early as an infant gazing into the irritated, unaccepting eyes of a disapproving parent. Perhaps the child was unplanned and unwanted, or perhaps they were outright rejected by their caretaker, usually a same-sex caretaker. This effectively brands the child as irrelevant and unwelcome. As the child grows, they start to believe more strongly that they are not wanted, and they try to disappear. They often wear the mask of the "runaway." This can even manifest in their physical form. They may be thin to the point of being skinny. Because they view themselves as unwanted, they feel awkward in the company of others, don't talk much, strive to be perfect because they've already been branded as unwelcome, and are constantly trying to prove they are worthy of love. They seek solace in solitude to avoid the stress of needing to show their worth constantly. They often look for an escape from their own anxiety through the abuse of various substances in hopes that it will help them disappear, become someone else, and/or just stop the pain.

2. Abandonment

This trauma often occurs from some type of abandonment by the opposite-sex parent. They may not have actually left the home, but they may have been distant or neglectful, and thus have emotionally abandoned the child.

Another female client of mine suffered from this trauma due to the aloofness of her father in the first four years of her life. Her father was a narcissist, and he had little to do with her early on. He didn't even visit her in the hospital as an infant. He abandoned her emotionally, and although her mother was a loving presence in her life, his abandonment resulted in numerous problems in her adult relationships. She became clingy to satisfy her hunger for her father's love, which he never gave her. She needed to have someone need her love and fell into codependency as a result. Her romantic partners, however, were subconsciously chosen for their similarities to her father, and to avoid having them abandon her, she often left them before they could leave her. It was a way to strike back at her father; however, it was never fulfilling, given that it wasn't actually her father. She always felt a void inside that she could never seem to fill until she was able to resolve the abandonment trauma she had suffered. Other manifestations of abandonment trauma include emotional dysregulation—laughing one minute and crying the next—dramatization, fear of loneliness, and depression. Physical displays include migraine headaches and asthma, among others.

3. Humiliation

This type of trauma results from an overly critical parenting style. It is particularly devastating for a child to hear criticism from their mother at a young age, although this type of wound can still occur at any age. This is a trauma with which I am very familiar. The humiliated child dons the mask of the masochist, which means they subconsciously look for problems and develop a low sense of self-worth from constant criticism and repeated humiliation. This, too, can result in codependency, as the sufferer strives to help others but then, voluntarily and subconsciously, becomes part of the problem, given that they are motivated out of fear and shame. This person is hypersensitive to criticism but often offends others without realizing it. Physical manifestations include back problems and respiratory diseases, out of feeling suffocated by the weight of their burden. Likewise, these individuals neglect their own needs in favor of helping others.

4. Betrayal

Betrayal is usually experienced when we are between the ages of two to four years old, and it is often the opposite-sex parent who perpetrates this trauma. This was another trauma suffered by my client, "Marie," whom I mentioned in the abandonment section. Her father often betrayed her trust by not keeping his word, seeming to prefer other people and emotionally abusing her. This type of trauma can cause an individual to become very controlling, which was true of Marie as well. She felt responsible for everything in her world and would strive to control herself, other people, and the circumstances in a given environment. She was extremely demanding of herself and others and was often disappointed when she or others failed to live up to her high standards. She would suffer an emotional breakdown when situations spiraled out of her control, and to prevent that from happening, she would not only come up with a Plan B, but also a Plan C, D, E, F, etc. Physical manifestations of betrayal trauma often come in the form of joint problems and digestive system issues. Marie had painful problems with her knees.

5. Injustice

This type of trauma usually occurs with the same-sex parent between the ages of three and five years old. This child has suffered a trauma that they have deemed unfair. A friend of mine suffered from this kind of trauma when her stepbrothers were taken from her family by their biological mother when she was just five years old. They had lived as one big happy family for two years, and suddenly, they were gone. It was all done due to the actions of adults without any consideration for the children. She experienced an injustice and, as a result, she put on a protective mask. She became rigidly perfectionist and was extraordinarily frustrated by those things she perceived were acting unfairly. For her, it was like she was experiencing her trauma all over again. Like anyone who suffers this kind of trauma, she was extremely hardworking, to the point of being a workaholic. But she would often exhaust herself to the point of a nervous breakdown. She lived in almost constant fear of making a mistake and disappointing other people. This would frequently cause her to lose sleep, which would become a major problem for her.

The 5 Traumas and Shadow Formation

As you might imagine, there are several opportunities for shadow formation when subjected to these kinds of trauma. An angry shadow may form, for example, with any of these traumas. The angry shadow tries to protect you from not only further trauma, but also your actions born as a result of the original trauma. For example, the client who suffered from abandonment trauma became codependent to fill a need for love. She related that she often felt "put upon" by her romantic partners who, being similar to her father, took advantage of her codependency. Although her shadow self harbored extreme resentment and anger toward these men, she feared expressing that anger because she didn't want them to leave her. That caused her to feel ashamed as well as angry at herself for being a "doormat." She couldn't express that anger, however, because anger was not socially acceptable and might endanger her relationship. Her angry self was her shadow self. It was a part of herself that she denied and hid from others and from herself.

My own rejection and humiliation from my mother resulted in low self-worth. I believed I was worthless and became a people-pleaser in an attempt to love myself. My mother's criticism made me fearful of making mistakes, and I became perfectionist as a result. I hid and rejected my lazy, bumbling shadow self because I saw it as imperfect and undesirable.

Likewise, people who experience the trauma of injustice hide their unfair shadow self from the world. They deny its existence because they know the pain of injustice and don't want to think they could ever treat others unfairly. This is one way we can recognize our shadow self. If there is someone who says or does something that bothers you, that's an indicator that your shadow self is seeking recognition. Can you think of how some of your pet peeves might indicate a hidden shadow? Maybe you feel overly bothered by someone who appears inefficient. That might indicate a lazy or inefficient shadow self. Perhaps it bothers you when someone wears something you consider inappropriate. You feel irritated by it to where you might even choose to say something about it. This could be because you are denying your "ugly" shadow self forged from an old rejection trauma you suffered. Your shadow self is something you don't want to believe is true about yourself. It's something you see as weak or unacceptable, and you can't accept it as a part of yourself. But every shadow brings a gift that can help us deal with those old traumas.

What is the Gift of the Shadow?

We deny their existence and bury them deep within our psyche because they often form as a result of trauma. But the shadow self is often the key to healing that trauma. In fact, it is only by accepting our shadow and acknowledging the gifts it brings that we can fully heal from those old wounds. How can you recognize the gifts of her shadow self? Let's look at a few examples.

- **Anger**—We are often taught by our families and society at large that anger is dangerous and should not be expressed. We reject it out of fear that it will cause us to be rejected or abandoned, humiliated or betrayed, or treated unfairly. But anger won't be denied, and as long as you express it healthily, it can help you set appropriate boundaries.
- **Imperfection**—Many of the traumas above can cause fear of imperfection. We don't want to be seen as flawed because we could be rejected, abandoned, or humiliated. But our imperfections help us cultivate self-compassion and self-forgiveness. When we can have compassion and forgiveness for ourselves, we can also express those sentiments for others.
- **Vulnerability**—Vulnerability is seen culturally and individually as a bad quality, one you don't want to possess. No one wants to be seen as vulnerable or weak. We push our perceived weaknesses deep inside. But being vulnerable opens us up to intimacy with others. Without the ability to be vulnerable and expose your weaknesses, it becomes very difficult to get close to another person.

So our shadow selves have valuable gifts to share with us, but to receive those gifts, we must first accept our shadow. To do that, we must heal the traumas that created them in the first place.

Exercise #6

You and Your Shadow

In this exercise, the goal is to help you identify the types of trauma you may have suffered in your own childhood, as well as the shadow selves you might have created as a result. Let's first look at the type of trauma you may have suffered.

Which Mask Do You Wear?

Circle the number that represents your experience the closest for each statement or question:

Which body type best describes your body?

- Skinny.
- Slender or normal, but lacking muscle tone.
- Plump or obese with a round face
- Strong body—in men, shoulders are wider than the lower body, and in women, the lower body is wider (pear-shaped).
- Well-proportioned but small and rigid.

Which of the following characterizes your behavior?

- You seek solitude and don't get attached to material things.
- You always need help and support, and your emotions are a roller coaster.
- You are messy, don't feel attractive, and reward yourself with food.
- You are uncompromising, interrupt others frequently, and are angered by inefficiency and laziness.
- You are a perfectionist but often doubt your choices; you can be short-tempered and have problems showing affection.

Which description best characterizes your relationships?

- You prefer solitude and don't speak up much in a group.
- You seek approval from others and have difficulty making decisions without their support.
- You do everything for others but blame yourself for everything as well, and even take the blame for other people.
- You have difficulty delegating tasks; you make backup plans for everything.
- You don't like to show your emotions, but you act to ensure others believe you deserve a reward.

Which of the following is true for you?

- You often use words like null, nothing, or disappear.
- You often use phrases like "I can't stand," "I'm being eaten…," or "I give up."
- You often use words like dignified, fat, dirty, unworthy, or pig.
- You often use phrases like "Let me do it," "Trust me," or "Do you understand."
- You often use words or phrases like "no problem," "always," "never," or "very good."

Which of the following would you say is your biggest fear?

- Panic
- Loneliness
- Freedom
- Disengagement, separation, dissociation, or denial
- Coldness

Once you have finished answering the questions, tally up your score. While there can be overlap, scores indicate the following:

- 5 - 8: Runaway mask associated with a wound of rejection.
- 9 - 12: Addict mask associated with a wound of abandonment.
- 13 - 17: Masochist mask associated with a wound of humiliation.
- 18 - 21: The Controller mask associated with a wound of betrayal.
- 22 - 25: The Rigid mask associated with a wound of injustice.

Although this is not a perfect system for identification of trauma, because you can suffer more than one trauma type, it should still give you a general idea of where you fall on the trauma scale. Once you have identified a type or types of trauma, reflect on its origins in a journal. This can help you further uncover old memories associated with traumatic events. Explore this old trauma as you feel is helpful for understanding your current behavior.

The Shadow Knows

The key to recognizing your shadow self lies in identifying what irks you the most. The things that trigger you often do so because you subconsciously believe them to be a part of yourself, and you have rejected that part. To find your shadow, you must delve into the depths of your psyche and explore what bothers you and why. Reflect on something that triggered you recently—something small that wasn't even associated with someone you know. Maybe you saw someone doing something and got very angry, or someone said something that you perceived negatively, and you judged that person harshly. Relive that experience in your mind as you reflect on the following prompts:

- What happened that bothered you?

- What did you perceive about the situation that made you judge those involved?
- What judgment did you make?
- What are your feelings about that—for example, if you judged them to be vain, why do you think vanity is so wrong, and can there be anything good about it?
- Can you remember the first time you felt judgmental about such a behavior or situation?
- Have you ever been judged in that way?
- Do you think you possess any level of that quality or trait?
- What would it mean if you did?

Write in as much detail as you can when responding to the prompts, but feel free to continue exploring your thoughts and emotions about this subject. Discovering the shadow and the trauma behind it is an important step toward healing.

Chapter 7

From Denial to Acceptance

Sometimes, it's very difficult to accept that you are codependent. After all, no one wants to admit that they are a people pleaser. Many times, they equate it with weakness, but that's not really what's going on. Codependency has little to do with your strength of character. It's all about the conditioning you received, both consciously and subconsciously, as a child. Still, the common perception is that you're somehow weak and obsequious. One client of mine, whom I'll call "Kate," gives a perfect example of this. She had suffered the traumas of rejection and abandonment by her father when she was young. Additionally, her codependent mother had modeled people-pleasing behaviors throughout her life. Moreover, her mother had tried to train her in codependency by telling her that it was her responsibility to take care of her disabled brother and younger sister. She was saddled with responsibility at a very young age, and as an adult, she saw herself as an independent, strong, and confident woman. She did indeed possess those qualities, but she had a history of failed relationships, and in each, she had been the one to leave. Her pattern was one of becoming involved with a man who was aloof and distant in some way, similar to her father. She would do many things for that man, but she would also push him to prove his love. Then, before he could leave, she would end the relationship. Her partners were often surprised by the way she ended things.

Finally, Kate met a man whom she actually married. By that time, she had realized her pattern of choosing men similar to her father and trying to relive that relationship with better results. But she thought she had finally broken the pattern. Unfortunately, although the man she married was very expressive of his love for her, he was also narcissistic just like her father. Over the course of their marriage, she had given in to his desires for things he wanted to do or have on many occasions, and this was despite the fact that she didn't want those things and didn't want to do what he did. Still, she saw that as evidence that she was a reasonable spouse who wasn't trying to control her husband. She wasn't a nag; she was an open, enlightened spouse. Because of her husband's choices and her support of those choices, the couple fell into financial problems. She was once again saddled with the lion's share of responsibility for supporting the family, this time financially. One day, her husband told her he had won a dinner with two nights and three days at a hotel. My client realized this was likely a sales tactic, and that when they went to the dinner, someone would try to sell them a timeshare or some other service. She mentioned this to her husband and told him that they were not going to buy anything they pitched, no matter how good it sounded.

Kate was correct about the sales pitch, but despite what she had said, her husband very much wanted to buy what they were selling. This time, however, she stood firm. She told him that she didn't know where they would come up with the extra money to pay for what this company was selling; since it would be her responsibility to pay, the answer was no. He grudgingly agreed and told them no sale. As they were going home, however, my client couldn't shake feeling upset that she had been unable to give her husband what he wanted. She felt like she had disappointed him. She explained that she experienced a sudden insight about herself that she had previously been denying—she was, in fact, codependent, and moreover, it was the result of long-term conditioning from her father's rejection and abandonment, in addition to her mother's training. She could suddenly see how she had introjected that sense that she was responsible for providing other people with what they wanted and needed, even if that came at her own expense. It was that insight and acceptance that was key to setting her free. Once she could see her own codependency and how it affected her behavior, she could take steps toward finally healing.

Acceptance is one of the most difficult things you'll ever do. But without acceptance, there can be no healing. You can't heal something that you don't accept as a reality. You have to see clearly and honestly what is going on to deal with it effectively. Acceptance is the final step in the stages of grief identified by a Swiss American psychiatrist, Elisabeth Kübler-Ross. The key to dealing with grief effectively, she determined, was by finally arriving at the stage of acceptance. Though she worked specifically on grief, we go through these same stages when dealing with any change or unexpected event. When working on your personal growth, you go through significant change and work through those changes by navigating the stages of grief. In a way, you are grieving. You're grieving the loss of the old, so you may celebrate the arrival of the new. Even if what you are leaving behind is something that no longer serves you, you go through a form of grief when transitioning to a new life. But how exactly do we go from denial to acceptance and heal codependency?

Moving Past Denial

The key to getting to acceptance is moving past denial. That's the first step in those five stages outlined by Kübler-Ross. From there, you would pass through the other stages of anger, bargaining, and depression before arriving at acceptance. When Kate reflected on her process of acceptance, she reflected on how she had passed through the other stages. She had initially denied her codependency, but after having her insights that fateful evening, she became very angry. She was angry at her mother and father for having saddled her with this condition. But more than that, she was angry with herself for allowing other people to take advantage of her for that long. It took some honest shadow work for her to embrace her people-pleasing shadow. She was able to do that when she embraced the gifts that that side of herself brought. After all, that part of her had good intentions. It wanted to help others and was just trying to help her love herself. Her shadow self was trying to help her find a way to cherish the kind, supportive person she truly was. Once she saw the gifts from the shadow, she was able to move past her anger.

From there, she moved on to bargaining with her people-pleasing tendencies. Perhaps there was a compromise she could make to please everyone, including herself. It didn't take long for Kate to see that wasn't going to work. There was no being just a little bit codependent. She had to prioritize her needs and desires and see that she was worthy of being prioritized. But that brought on the depression associated with feeling like she was losing herself somewhere along the way. She expressed not really knowing who she had been all those years and who she was becoming now. But when she finally accepted what happened to her, she was able to move on from her codependent behavior. She could finally free herself of the burden of having to make everyone happy. She realized that she wasn't responsible for saving anyone other than herself. She wasn't responsible for anyone else's happiness, nor for providing for them either. She found that her life became much better all around as a result of these changes. Because she respected herself, the people around her also began to see her in a new light. They began to respect her, even though she wasn't giving them everything they wanted anymore. That made it much easier for her to cultivate her self-worth. This is the value of this healing strategy, and it exemplifies the importance of acceptance.

Seeing the Patterns

One of the most important facets of moving from denial to acceptance is taking an honest look at your behavioral patterns through the years. Usually, this is prompted by something that has happened. It's something that causes you to finally realize that something's got to give. If you're not in some level of pain, it's unlikely that you'll begin to move through the cycle of acceptance. Let's take a look at this cycle and how you might experience it.

Normal Life

Initially, you're going through your normal life. You're functioning well enough, and although you have some inner turmoil, it's not painful enough to prompt real change. For Kate, she had settled into her married life, and though she felt some level of discontent, it wasn't enough to cause any real movement.

The Pain Becomes Unbearable

The next stage in the cycle is that of the pain increasing to an unbearable level for some reason. In Kate's case, this happened when her mother passed away and left her with the responsibility of caring for her sister. Her sister had a personality disorder that her mother had enabled for the majority of her life. Her sister's learned helplessness was such that it was incapacitating. Her mother had left her with that huge responsibility. It was bad news that significantly increased the pain of her inner turmoil.

Then Comes Denial

Kate had long been in denial of her codependency, but she had also denied that her mother had been somehow at fault for the situation.

She couldn't believe it was true; she didn't *want* to believe it was true. But the closer she looked, the more her denial crumbled away.

The Anger Stage

The next step in the process is anger. Kate was incredibly angry at her situation. She was angry at her sister and mother for putting her in this situation. Although she raged to herself privately, she didn't express this anger to those who were deserving of it. She even had trouble admitting her anger toward her mother, since she was now deceased. But she finally let herself feel that anger and expressed it. That was a breakthrough that led to the next stage.

Depression is Up Next

Initially, Kate was depressed because she felt overwhelmed and trapped. She didn't see any way out of the situation her mother had put her in. She didn't want to let her sister become homeless or have to be committed any more than her mother had wanted. Initially, all she could see was that she would have to take on this enormous, unfair responsibility.

Bargaining for a Solution

After that, Kate began to bargain for an acceptable solution. She had several ideas of what she might do that would take care of her sister's needs without her actually having to live with her. They all involved her taking on burdens that were not hers to bear. And they all required her continuing codependency.

Acceptance at Last

Finally, Kate arrived at the stage of acceptance. She accepted the problem for what it was, and she accepted both her mother's and her own role in creating it. That led to her realizing that she was, in fact, codependent. And when she finally could see that truth about herself, she could then take the steps she needed to heal. This is true for all of us. We see the world through the lens of our trauma, and to resolve those old wounds, we often unconsciously create repetitive scenarios in our lives that approximate the wounding relationship. It becomes like the metaphor in Don Quixote of fighting the windmills; it's an endless cycle such that it seems there is no way out. In reality, our traumas create illusions that obscure our vision. To see clearly, we have to accept the situation we are in and the reasons behind it. When that happens, it'll be as if we have finally removed the blinders preventing us from seeing clearly. We can then realize the mask we have donned and why. That's the first step toward healing.

So, what patterns have you seen in your own life? Do you have a history of troubled relationships? Does it feel overwhelming with certain responsibilities? What is your role in creating or perpetuating that situation? When you look back at cycles that involve the grief process, it can help you to identify those patterns. It's also helpful if you can explore your normal reactions to the grief cycle. For example, when you become angry, how do you typically express that anger? Do you fly off the handle or hold your anger inside? Maybe you even turn it inward toward yourself to avoid taking it out on someone else. This is a common pattern for codependents. In some ways, they work as hard at image control as toxic people do. They don't want people to see their anger or dissatisfaction, so they bury it and try to deal with those difficult emotions without appearing too expressive. In that way, they can continue to please the people in their life.

This was the battle that I fought in my own life. My mother was very critical, and I tried so hard to please her so she would love me, which would then give me permission to love myself. This is the struggle of the codependent—it's really what you're looking for, the sense of self-worth you need to love yourself. The problem is that you're delegating that power to someone else. You're looking for love in all the wrong places, as the song goes. Self-love cannot be found through anyone else, but the wounded self-esteem of the codependent can't see that. In one sense, they can't even see themselves anymore. Their whole life is geared toward pleasing other people; it feels as though they don't matter. It is through service to others that they find their self-worth, but self-worth must grow from within to be a healthy part of your identity. It's not something external that you can acquire; it's something you cultivate from self-love.

Exercise #7

What are Your Patterns?

As with the other exercises we've done, there are two parts to this exercise. The first is identifying your patterns, and the second is identifying your pain. Let's start with the patterns.

Lifelong Patterns

Begin by answering the prompts below, and then reflect on the patterns you see and what created them. What is the reason you do what you do? What makes you like certain things? What triggers you into making the choices you make?

- What kind of characteristics do you find attractive in a potential mate?
- How many intimate relationships have you had in your life?
- How long do your relationships typically last?
- Are you the one who ends those relationships, or does someone else?

- When you're in a relationship, do you normally make the rules in the household, or do you follow someone else's rules?
- How do you feel when you tell someone no?
- Do you work outside of the home? If so, what kind of work do you do?
- Do you prefer to be the boss or the employee?
- How do you feel if you can't do something someone has asked you to do?
- Do you worry that people won't like you if you don't do what they want?

After you've answered these questions, explore your answers a little more by noting the patterns you see and what they might mean to you. Can you identify specific reasons behind your behaviors? For example, if you have had several intimate relationships, but they don't last very long, can you identify a reason why? Are you afraid of getting too close? Do you sabotage those relationships? Write as much or as little as you need to in order to better understand your patterns of behavior. You're taking the blinders off to see clearer. To do that, you need to understand yourself better.

What Brought You Here?

The next step in this exercise is to explore your pain. You've arrived at reading this book for a reason. Something has prompted you to explore the roots of your behavior. What happened? Why did you take this significant step? Did you suffer the loss of a loved one, as Kate did? Did you break up with someone for the umpteenth time? Are you starting to think, "Maybe it's me?" What was the event or realization that prompted you to look for answers? I know I say it a lot, but write about it. When you write, you may gain insights you may not otherwise have. Let yourself explore where your writing goes; it may show you the way. From this point, we can start to explore what happens next.

Chapter 8

So You're Codependent—What Now?

When I realized my codependency, I knew I was going to have to face some very difficult emotions. I knew I would need the courage to dive into my past and explore my trauma. I knew this wasn't going to be easy, and it wasn't going to be a quick fix, but the hardest part was over. I had accepted my codependency, and that's when the healing began. There are a number of healing strategies you can employ for codependency. I'll discuss specific strategies in my next book on this subject, *Healing Codependency: How to Resolve Your Childhood Trauma so You Can Start Living Your Best Life,* but now you have some tools you can use for better insight into the problem. Let's explore a few more ideas to get you started.

Make a List and Check It Twice

The first step after realizing you're codependent is identifying your codependent behaviors. Once you've done that, you can determine the behaviors you want to achieve. Remember—you can't fix anything until you know what's wrong. My codependent behaviors consisted of subconsciously choosing partners similar to my mother so that I could "fix" the damaged relationship we had when I was a child. Now, you might think that I could just go talk to my mother and fix it that way. But the fundamental problem with trying to fix anything that happened in the past is that it already happened. Even if you can express your anger and pain to the person who wounded you, you can't undo the wound that way. Even if they acknowledge that they acted harshly or cruelly, that doesn't undo the harm they did. You've already incorporated that wound into your identity. That's also the problem with trying to fix a damaged relationship from your past through finding a similar partner. Even if I had chosen someone like my mother and convinced them to change, I would still have a wounded inner child who needed my attention.

Another behavior of mine that I identified was that I was always taking responsibility for the well-being of other people. Like Kate, I thought it was my responsibility to make other people happy. This is an attempt to love myself by pouring my love into someone else. When they return my love, it's as if I am giving myself love. But it's not the same, and it never will be. In fact, you can't really love someone else the way they deserve until you can love yourself. Moreover, it can cause a lack of boundaries. By taking on the responsibility of making someone else happy, I have to know their most private thoughts and desires. I have to be receiving feedback constantly. If they express any level of discomfort, I must act immediately to assuage the problem. It's an impossible task, and it's not my job. It also requires that I violate their boundaries and don't establish any of my own. I have never had boundaries because it's not something my mother would allow. I never learned what boundaries were until I began my own healing process. Now I can see how my codependency prevented healthy boundary formation, and it also prevented me from respecting other people's boundaries.

By taking on the responsibility for someone else's well-being and happiness, I was also creating another codependent behavior: an overreliance on someone else meeting my needs. I was looking to love myself, and to do that, I needed them to love me. In that way, I was relying on *them* to satisfy *my* need for something that only *I* could provide for myself. It's a situation that will never feel satisfying. I, like most codependents, feel a constant void inside—a yawning, empty hole that only genuine self-love can ever fill. Thus, no matter what I did or how much my partner seemed to love me, I never felt satisfied. I never felt like I was enough. Moreover, because I was so reliant on their feedback, I became hypervigilant of any changes in communication. If they seemed quiet, I interpreted that as them having stopped loving me. If they were angry, it must've been at me. If they were sad, I needed to entertain them. It was quite simply exhausting, and my self-esteem suffered because I could never get it right, just as I had never gotten it right in my mother's eyes. Here are some other codependent behaviors.

- Caretaking to the point of neglecting your own needs.
- Reacting emotionally rather than rationally.
- Feeling like you lost yourself.
- Feeling like you need to do whatever it takes to make someone else happy.
- A persistent feeling of emptiness that drives your service.

What are your characteristics of codependency? Think carefully about your behavioral patterns and write down the ones that might indicate codependency.

What Do You Want to Achieve?

The next part of identifying your codependent patterns is thinking carefully about what exactly you hope to achieve by doing this work. Something brought you here to learn more about codependency. What was the breaking point for you? What was the pain that became so great that you just had to act? And how do you hope learning about this behavioral pattern will alleviate the pain? Remember that for Kate, the breaking point was the death of her mother and the looming responsibility of caring for her sister. For me, it was yet another failed relationship. Similar to an alcoholic, codependents will often hit "rock bottom." That is the point at which the pain becomes so great that they can no longer ignore it.

Essentially, you are forced to act, and although you might not think that learning more about the problem is acting, it's the first and most significant step in the journey toward healing. But to understand what to do next, you have to identify your goals. For most codependents, the ultimate goal is learning to love oneself and understanding their inherent value as distinct from anything they do in life. I am not valued based on my ability to maintain a relationship. Kate is not valued based on her ability to care for her sister. You are not valued based on your ability to please anyone other than yourself.

How do you achieve that sense of self-worth? It starts with identifying your behavioral patterns and then your goals for healing. For Kate, she wanted to be free of her self-worth being measured by how successful she could be at taking care of her sister and pleasing her mother. That's a heavy burden. For me, my goal was learning to love myself so I could love someone else for who they were. When you free yourself of that emptiness and replace that void with knowing you can be loved and supported no matter what, only then can you love someone else. You can genuinely want the best for them, even if that means they are not with you. Codependency is the opposite of that. They have to be with you because that's where you derive your self-love. If they leave, you will be abandoned yet again. In other words, you try to force them to be happy so you will feel happy and satisfied, but of course, that can't work. True happiness is grown from within. You have to break that habit of looking for an external source of self-worth and self-love. When you can do that, you can break free of the resulting behaviors tied to your search for fulfillment.

Breaking the patterns means first recognizing them, then replacing them with healthier habits. So let's look at a few ways you break out of the rigid patterns that guided your life to date.

❖ Change the View

As a codependent, you're accustomed to thinking of other people before yourself. To heal, you have to start changing your focus. Destructive self-neglect is one of the hallmarks of codependency, so you need to identify the needs you have been neglecting in favor of serving others.

This means looking inward and identifying exactly what you need. I needed time alone and therapy to process my patterns and break them. Kate needed distance from her overly attached mother and father. What do you need? Write it down.

❖ Find Yourself

When I began identifying what I needed, I was genuinely frightened about talking to my mother or anyone else about what I wanted for myself. I was so used to saying something like, "I'm good with whatever you decide," that I rarely ever voiced my opinion, even for something as simple as stating what I wanted to eat for dinner.

Codependents often fear voicing their desires because they are afraid they might upset someone around them. They don't want to be seen as selfish, but it's not selfish to state your preferences. You can practice this by starting with simple things. I began by saying, "I want Italian food tonight."

It seems like such a small step, but as Lao Tzu said, "A journey of a thousand miles begins with a single step." That first small step will lead you to the second, and the third, until you arrive at your goal. Identify a first step toward refocusing on yourself.

❖ Identify Your Limits

The next step is to identify your boundaries. This doesn't mean identifying what you won't do to please someone. It means identifying the boundaries you have for respecting yourself.

Boundaries are not about trying to get someone else to respect you; they are about respecting yourself. To identify my boundaries, I would think about times when I was hurt by someone, either by something they said or did. As I thought about those incidents, I could think about what made me feel disrespected by their actions.

For example, when my mother criticized me unfairly, I felt unloved. I also felt undervalued. Love and value were what I believed she was not giving me. She was crossing a line in failing to do so because she was my mother.

Another example comes from a friend of mine whose husband has a tendency to minimize her work. He constantly interrupts her workday to ask her to do something for him, and she's codependent too. What he was failing to respect was her contribution to the family's financial support. He was crossing a boundary.

Once you recognize your boundaries, you can protect them. For example, my friend would simply say to her husband, "I'm sorry. I can't do that right now. When I finish work, I can try to help." That was one small step toward respecting her contribution enough to say no.

I'll talk much more about how to identify, set, and protect your boundaries in my next book. For now, just try to identify boundaries and what you believe is lacking when someone violates them.

It Takes Time and Commitment

You've taken the first, and in some ways, the most important steps toward identifying your codependency patterns. You've accepted your codependency, and now, it's time to take action toward healing those old wounds and move into a better future. As you go down this road, it's important to remember that it takes time and commitment. You have to stick to your priorities of self-care, self-reflection, and processing the toxicity from external sources. This is the only way to heal. There are times when you may feel depressed; it's one of those grief stages we discussed before. But if you take the time to sit with your feelings and understand them, you will also begin to notice that those feelings shift; they are not forever. You will move from depression to the next stages until you reach acceptance. A common feature of the codependent personality is perfectionism. Codependents believe they have to get everything just perfect, or it's a reflection of what a failure they are, but you have to let that go. There is no such thing as perfect. Everything and everyone is a work in progress.

An important part of staying committed to your healing journey is self-awareness. This means you have to focus on your own feelings to understand how they are affecting your behavior. You need to process the times when you don't feel right about something. People often don't want to look at the reasons behind their behavior or feelings because they fear it will reveal something inherently bad about themselves. Nothing could be further from the truth. You are not inherently bad; you've just been conditioned to perform a certain way. Now, it's time to undo that conditioning because it's no longer serving you. When I was a confused, helpless child, my codependency was a survival mechanism. It got me through those difficult times. But now, I don't need it anymore. In fact, I know now that I need to prioritize my own needs and desires. That's where you are. Your codependency doesn't serve you anymore. It's time for new habits and a new path—a path toward healing old wounds and moving on to the life you want. You're a courageous person for undertaking such a journey, but you're not alone. Together, we can strive for a happier, healthier tomorrow.

Exercise #8

Mindfulness Meditation for Self-Awareness

One of the most important things you can do at this stage is to cultivate mindfulness and build self-awareness. You've been doing several exercises related to reflecting on your situation of codependency, and it's important to stay mindful while you do those. You may experience several emotions as you go through this process, and to advance your healing, you'll need to be aware of the changes you're going through, so you can process your feelings and make the best decisions on how to proceed. Meditation is one of the best techniques you can use for that purpose. It's important to cultivate a relationship with your body, thoughts, and feelings. After all, you've been denying your needs for so long that it's a strong habit to overcome. By re-engaging your awareness with your body and emotional changes, you can be aware of your needs in the present moment, so you can address them when they arise. This meditation exercise will help you to make that long journey from your mind to your heart.

To begin, you want to arrange for a place that is quiet and where you can be comfortable and undisturbed. It's helpful to make it into a real place of your own. You might place scented candles, comfortable seating, and appropriate lighting in this area. You'll also want to let anyone in your life know that when you're in this location, you are not to be disturbed. When you have this set up, it's a good idea to make a regular schedule for practicing your meditation. You don't have to meditate for a long time; even just a few minutes each day can help you make that connection between mind and body. You'll also want to have your journal stored in this location so you can write about any insights you experience. Once you're ready to meditate, set up the room accordingly, get seated comfortably, and allow yourself to relax. One final note before we begin—you don't have to sit cross-legged or in a lotus position for this to work. You can sit or even lie down, but you want to be in a position where you can remain alert. You don't want to fall asleep during this exercise. Now that you're comfortable and set up, let's move this guided meditation. If you would prefer, you can also record your voice, or someone else's soothing voice reading through this guided meditation, and then, you can play it back while meditating.

1. Get comfortable and close your eyes.
2. Take 10 deep breaths that expand both your stomach and your chest. Breathe in through your nose and out through your mouth.
3. Bring your attention to your breath and follow it as it enters through your nostrils, passes down the back of your throat, and expands your lungs. Count to four as you inhale.
4. Once your lungs are expanded, hold that breath and count to four again.
5. Exhale slowly to a count of eight. Follow your breath as it empties from your lungs, passes through your throat and into your mouth, and exits from your body.
6. Now, bring your focus to the top of your head. Notice any sensations you feel there. Does something itch? Does something tickle? Does something hurt? Can you feel a hat or anything else you have on your head?
7. If there is an area of pain, breathe deeply into that spot.
8. Move down your body to the back of your head, face, and neck. Notice any areas of pain, itchiness, or tickling. Breathe into anything that is uncomfortable.
9. From there, move down to your arms. Can you feel your hands resting on your lap or on the floor? Can you feel the cloth of the shirt you have on? Do you feel any areas of pain or discomfort? Breathe into any such areas.

10. If your mind wanders during this process, just notice it and where it goes. Did you think about what you might make for dinner? That's planning. Did you worry about your bills? That's worrying. Whatever kind of thought you have when your mind wanders, label it as to the type, and then envision it wafting above your head and dissipating into the air, in the same way smoke rises from a campfire and dissipates into the sky above. Then gently and without judgment bring your focus back to your body.
11. Continue to move down into each area of your body—your chest, abdomen, pelvic region, legs, and feet. As before, notice any areas of discomfort and breathe into those areas. Be aware of the sensations you experience as you go through this process. Notice any change in your emotions and any thoughts you have.
12. Once you have moved through your entire body, bring your awareness back to your breath.
13. Take 10 more deep, belly and chest-expanding breaths, inhaling through the nose to a count of four, holding your breath for a count of four, and then exhaling through your mouth to a count of eight.
14. Thank your body for all it does for you, and thank yourself for taking care of your needs.
15. When you're ready, open your eyes.

Do this meditation several times, focusing solely on your body. Reflect in your journal about the sensations you experienced and the many ways in which your body tried to distract you from your mindfulness practice. You'll find you suddenly have an itch, for example, and it might even feel intense while you're meditating. This is your body's way of distracting you. Try not to move or scratch that itch; just notice how the sensation changes. The more you can sit with the sensations, the more your body will calm down during this practice. As we move on to healing, you'll use this meditation as a good springboard for exploring your deeper feelings and old wounding experiences that caused your codependence. For now, just become accustomed to the practice and make it a habit. You'll soon find that you can bring yourself into the present moment, even when you're not meditating. This will help you stay calm and think carefully about how to respond to stressful situations. It's a useful practice for managing stress as you go down the road to a solution.

Chapter 9

The Road to a Solution – First Steps

You've taken the first steps, and now you know much more about how codependence forms and how the patterns in your life shaped it. It's extremely important to take a moment to congratulate yourself for the difficult work you've done. Celebrate how you've recognized that your needs *do* matter. That's what drew you to this book and the work we're doing here. You are a brave soul, and you're not alone. There are many people struggling with the same kinds of difficulties you've been experiencing your whole life. That's an important fact to know because often, the abusers of codependents have led them to believe the problem is with them. They are to blame, and no one else behaves that way; that's what they will tell you, but that's a lie. The people who have tried to make you feel responsible are doing so because they have an agenda. They are manipulators, and they want you to need them. That's sad, but it's natural that you might want to help them. They do have a problem, but it's not your job to fix it. I know I was all about helping my mother. It was so important to me to save her from the difficult life we were enduring. If you love someone, that's naturally what you want to do. But it wasn't my job, and it's not your job either.

- You have a right to have your needs met.
- You have a right to have your desires fulfilled.
- You have a right to focus on your own needs.

- You have a right to prioritize your own desires.
- You have a right to make your own choices.
- You have a right to respect and kindness.
- You have a right to love and be loved.
- You have a right to live YOUR life.
- You have a right to be independent.
- You have a right to be free of destructive criticism.
- You have a right to respect.
- You have a right to have other people consider your needs too, even as they focus on their own.
- You have a right to be free of toxic people.
- You have a right to know that you are valuable.
- You have a right to self-compassion.
- You have a right to self-love.
- You have a right to self-forgiveness.
- You have a right to self-worth.
- You have a right to a happy life.

These statements represent your new Bill of Rights. Feel free to add as many as are relevant to your life. This is your commitment to move forward with your personal growth. This is your recognition that you are a valuable, unique, beautiful, and loving soul whose contributions are important and make a difference. This is your declaration of your intention to heal.

From this point, the next steps involve moving forward in the healing process. You've recognized the problem and are committed to solving it. Now, you're turning your attention to the healing work that will repair the damage done by years of emotional and possibly physical abuse. In my next book, *Healing Codependency: How to Resolve Your Childhood Trauma so You Can Start Living Your Best Life,* I will guide you step-by-step through proven techniques for healing your codependency. These are the techniques that worked for me, so I know they can help you, too. Together, we can step into the happier, healthier life that is waiting for us. You can heal, and you can become a strong, independent, and happy person. In this book, I'll take show you:

- How to determine the people and situations who contributed to your codependency.
- How to identify the wounds they created and the emotional triggers that resulted.
- How to defuse those triggers as you embrace your shadow self and rebirth your inner child.
- How to save yourself as you resolve any old, toxic relationships that have been holding you down.
- How to build new, healthy habits to preserve your newfound independence.
- How to keep it real as you face new challenges in life.

You have what you need inside of yourself to heal. All you need now is someone to show you the way. You've already come so far, and there's no turning back now. Welcome to your new life that's just waiting for you to live it. Today is the day you start prioritizing yourself. It is my honor to be by your side as you go through the process. Please feel free to reach out with any comments or questions you have. Here is my Facebook page www.facebook.com/elena.miro.psy. I would also love to hear from you regarding your progress.

I am so honored that you chose my book and trusted me with your time. This is the most valuable thing any of us has, and it is my most sincere intention to make sure you feel your time has been well-spent reading this book. Sometimes, personal growth seems like an invisible process, but if you stick to it, you will wake up one day and find that you are living a happier, healthier life in line with your integrity and dreams. This happened in my life, and I know it will happen for you too. Remember, you are not alone on this journey of healing. Many people walk alongside you, including me. We help each other, and toward that end, it will also help me tremendously if you could leave a review or rating. I know you may be busy, but it will not only help me; it will let other people know that you found the content valuable.

Thank you.

Kind regards,

Elena Miro

References Cited

A Brief Overview of Adult Attachment Theory and Research | R. Chris Fraley. (n.d.).

http://labs.psychology.illinois.edu/~rcfraley/attachment.htm

Bortolon, C. B., Signor, L., De Campos Moreira, T., Figueiró, L. R., Benchaya, M. C., Machado, C. A., Ferigolo, M., & Barros, H. M. T. (2016). Family functioning and health issues associated with codependency in families of drug users. Ciência E Saúde Coletiva, 21(1), 101–107

https://doi.org/10.1590/1413-81232015211.20662014.

Coffman, E., & Swank, J. (2021). Attachment Styles and the Family Systems of Individuals Affected by Substance Abuse. The Family Journal, 29(1), 102–108. https://doi.org/10.1177/1066480720934487.

Dependent Personality Disorder DSM-5 301.6 (F60.7) - Therapedia. (n.d.).

https://www.theravive.com/therapedia/dependent-personality-disorder-dsm--5-301.6-(f60.7).

Family Life Matters: Combating Codependency. (n.d.). www.army.mil.

https://www.army.mil/article/137572/family_life_matters_combating_codependency#:~:text=Children%20who%20are%20raised%20to,American%20population%20demonstrates%20codependent%20behavior.

Gordon RM, Spektor V, Luu L (2019) Personality Organization Traits and Expected Countertransference and Treatment Interventions. Int J Psychol Psychoanal 5:039. doi.org/10.23937/2572-4037.1510039.

Knapek E, Kuritárné Szabó I. A kodependencia fogalma, tünetei és a kialakulásában szerepet játszó tényezők [The concept, the symptoms and the etiological factors of codependency]. Psychiatr Hung. 2014;29(1):56-64. Hungarian. PMID: 24670293.

Main, M., & Solomon, J. (1986). Discovery of an insecure-disorganized/disoriented attachment pattern. In T. B. Brazelton & M. W. Yogman (Eds.), *Affective development in infancy* (pp. 95–124). Ablex Publishing.

Mcleod, S., PhD. (2023). Erik Erikson's 8 Stages of Psychosocial Development. Simply Psychology. https://www.simplypsychology.org/erik-erikson.html.

Mikulincer M, Shaver PR. An attachment perspective on psychopathology. *World Psychiatry*. 2012 Feb;11(1):11-5. doi: 10.1016/j.wpsyc.2012.01.003. PMID: 22294997; PMCID: PMC3266769.

Salomonsson, B. (2018). Psychodynamic Interventions in Pregnancy and Infancy: Clinical and Theoretical Perspectives. Routledge.

https://www.taylorfrancis.com/chapters/mono/10.4324/9781351117142-4/delivery-trauma-maternal-introject-bj%C3%B6rn-salomonsson.

Sjöblom M, Öhrling K, Prellwitz M, Kostenius C. Health throughout the lifespan: The phenomenon of the inner child reflected in events during childhood experienced by older persons. Int J Qual Stud Health Well-being. 2016 Jun 16;11:31486. doi: 10.3402/qhw.v11.31486. PMID: 27317381; PMCID: PMC4912602.

Subramanian, S., & Dewaram Francis Raj, I. (2012). The efficacy of an intervention on healing the inner child on emotional intelligence, and adjustment among the college students. Indian Journal of Health and Wellbeing, 3(3), 648–652.

https://ischolar.in/index.php/ijhw/article/viewFile/49460/40464.

Tonik Web Studio. (n.d.). Lise Bourbeau. Lise Bourbeau. https://www.lisebourbeau.com/en/.

Book 2

Healing Codependency

Chapter 1

Who Built You?

We often talk about building our houses or even our lives, but there are ways in which our lives—our childhood home and experiences—also build us. Construction begins with your very first breath and experiencing the world around you. Of course, it can also be argued that you first learn about the world while you're still nestled in your mother's womb. Her fears infuse your newly forming body with an estimate of what the world will be like when you arrive. Research has found, in fact, that the uterine environment is a dynamic place wherein the mother and fetus are in a constant state of communication and adjustment. Even at such a tender state of development, construction has begun on the unique entity that will become you. However, after you're born, that process accelerates. In my first book on codependency, *Am I a People Pleaser? Codependency and the Childhood Trauma that Creates Relationship Addicts*, I discussed attachment theory and how you form your foundational perspective of the world around you in the first two to three years of your life. Let me give you a brief overview.

You can think of attachment theory as analogous to the childhood story of the *Three Little Pigs*. Attachment theory relates to how you come to view the world. It's your foundation for how you will proceed when making certain choices. People whose mothers or other primary caregivers respond to their needs quickly and satisfyingly develop secure attachment styles. Their choices are born from a foundation wherein they believe that the world is a safe place where their needs will usually be met, and they respond to crises in accordance with that belief. They have been built into a solid house of brick by the people and experiences around them. When the wolf comes to their door, he can huff and puff all he likes, but he won't be able to blow their house down. That sounds like magical thinking to someone like me, who developed an insecure attachment style. People whose primary caregivers were slow to meet their needs or perhaps neglected them altogether may view the world as unsafe and unable to meet their needs. This is where I live, and I don't live there alone; most with codependency have an insecure attachment style. The basis for our choices comes from a place of fear and insecurity. The experiences and people who built us weren't careful in their construction techniques; they cut corners and used straw and wood for materials. The most fearful among us are constructed of straw, and the wolf is easily able to blow us over. Some of us are made of wood, but the wolf can still blow us over with a little more energy. This is the basis for many psychological problems, including patterns of codependent behaviors. But let's go deeper yet—into the human psyche.

The Birth of Desire: Sigmund Freud and the Human Psyche

According to psychologist Sigmund Freud, the human psyche is made up of three parts: the Id, the Ego, and the Super-ego.

The Id is basically the primitive, instinctual part of our mind. It includes our libido—or sexual drives—as well as our aggressive drives. It also includes our hidden memories. The Super-ego is our moral compass. It is the part of our mind that incorporates the values and morals we learn from our parents and our culture. It is the part of us that doles out rewards in the form of, for example, feelings of pride or satisfaction; likewise, it also meets out punishment, manifested as emotions like shame and guilt. Finally, the Ego is the part of our mind that mediates between the primitive desires of the Id and the moral guidelines of the Super-ego. The Id is impulsive and infantile and changes little over time. It does not operate on logic—it is best described as fantasy-oriented. The Ego is the only part of this trio that we are consciously aware of; it is what we think of when we think of ourselves. It is the decision-making component of our mind that operates on the reality principle as it tries to satisfy both the baser urges of the Id and the strict moral codes of the Super-ego.

The Super-ego includes two systems: the conscience and the ideal self. These aspects of the self are what a person would use to push toward perfection. The conscience tells us when we've done something wrong; the ideal self encompasses the mental construct of who you aspire to be, which includes an intricate portrayal that encompasses your professional ambitions, perspectives on how you treat others, and the expectations of societal behavior.

We incorporate the norms taught by our parents and the society in which we live into our Super-ego, which then acts as our moral compass. It's not something we're necessarily consciously aware of, although if asked, we can certainly recite our moral norms. That doesn't mean, however, that we can fully understand how they are guiding our behavior. Regardless of societal norms, each of us harbors a primordial essence—a fundamental element woven into the very fabric of our consciousness—comprising our instincts and untamed desires, which have been indelibly imprinted over countless ages of evolutionary influence.

This is the Id—it encompasses the behaviors and drives that have contributed to individual generational success, thus resulting in a thriving population well-adapted to their environment. As humans, our environment includes the whole world; thus, our range of successful behaviors, and their subsequent instinctual drives, can be quite broad. We are rarely aware of drives beyond insatiable urges or desires. You might, for example, have an insatiable desire for sugar. You know you want it every time you see it, and even at times when you don't. You might attribute it to the addictive nature of processed sugar, but it actually goes back to a basic, evolutionarily guided drive. In our distant ancestors who were forced to live off the land and suffered from seasonal starvation, sugar was a rare albeit valuable resource due to its high caloric content. As a result, [humans evolved a "thrifty gene"](#) that codes sugar cravings, so when it is available, they would eat all that they could get, which would then give them stored fat to carry them through lean times. Now, in an age of overabundance, it is causing problems like obesity and diabetes. Knowing that doesn't kill the craving, however. It's a desire that's been coded in your genes and manifested in your Id beyond the ages.

Between these two mechanisms—the Super-ego and the Id—there is the Ego. This is your conscious awareness of self. Though conscious, it's still guided by unconscious forces working through the Super-ego and the Id; the Ego strives to mediate the two. You can view it as the mediator bargaining between two parties in a lawsuit. The Super-ego demands adherence to a certain moral code, whereas the Id wants what it wants, and it wants it *now!* The Ego tries to appease both sides. You can already probably see numerous ways in which this system might go awry, particularly in a dysfunctional family environment where extremes are the norm. As a codependent, you are torn by your Id's primitive, instinctual need for human connection—the result of generations of evolutionary forces at work on a social organism—and the values instilled in your Super-ego by the people and experiences who built you. So who were they, and what kind of materials did they use?

The Blueprint to Build You

The blueprint for building you began with your first interactions with your primary caregivers. Whether or not they mirrored loving, caring emotions or neglectful, negative emotions, that all formed the basis for your first impressions of the world. Mirroring is imitating or reflecting the emotions, expressions, and behaviors of another person. It is a natural and essential part of human communication and social interaction. Mirroring plays a crucial role in the development of infants, as it helps them form secure attachments, learn social skills, and build self-awareness. Attachment is, as we have discussed, the emotional bond that forms between an infant and their primary caregiver, usually a mother. Attachment provides the infant with a sense of security, comfort, and trust. Mirroring is one way that caregivers can foster attachment with their infants. By mirroring the infant's facial expressions, vocalizations, and movements, the caregiver shows that they are attentive, responsive, and empathetic to the infant's needs and feelings. This creates a positive feedback loop that reinforces the attachment bond. Mirroring also helps the infant regulate their emotions and cope with stress. For example, when an infant cries, the caregiver can mirror their distress, and then soothe them with a calm voice and a gentle touch. This shows the infant that they are not alone and that their emotions are valid and manageable.

Learning in infants is acquiring new knowledge, skills, and abilities through observation, imitation, and feedback. Learning is essential for the survival and adaptation of infants in their environment, particularly for pre-verbal infants. Mirroring facilitates learning by providing infants with models to imitate and feedback to improve. By mirroring the actions and words of their caregivers and others around them, infants learn how to perform various tasks and communicate effectively. For example, when an infant sees their caregiver smiling and saying "hello," they can mirror their expression and sound and learn how to greet someone. Mirroring also helps infants to learn about cause and effect, social norms, and moral values; when an infant sees their caregiver reacting positively or negatively to certain behaviors, they can mirror their emotion and learn what is acceptable or unacceptable. This is a vital step in eventually developing identity.

Identity is the perception of oneself that evolves gradually as a result of developing self-awareness, self-recognition, and self-esteem, and is important for the psychological well-being and social integration of infants. Mirroring supports identity development by offering infants feedback on themselves and their relationships. Through mirroring in a mirror or camera, caregivers aid infants in recognizing their distinct individuality, fostering self-awareness and self-recognition. Additionally, caregivers can nurture infants' positive self-image and self-esteem by mirroring their qualities and accomplishments in a supportive and encouraging manner. This then fosters self-confidence and self-respect. Moreover, mirroring is beneficial not only for infants, but also for caregivers, as it enhances their emotional connection, mutual understanding, and satisfaction with their relationship. Mirroring also contributes to introjection.

Introjection is a psychological process in which a person unconsciously incorporates the attitudes, values, or behaviors of another person or group into their own self-concept. Introjection can be seen as a form of identification, but it differs from identification in that it involves a passive and uncritical acceptance of external influences rather than an active and selective assimilation of them. Introjection can have both positive and negative effects on your personality and mental health, depending on the nature and source of the introjected material. One of the main functions of introjection is to protect the ego from anxiety or guilt by internalizing the standards and expectations of others. For example, a child who is scolded by their parents for doing something wrong may introject their parents' voices and repeat the same criticism to themselves whenever they make a mistake. Doing so can help the child avoid further punishment and conform to social norms, but it can also lead to low self-esteem and excessive self-criticism in adulthood. Similarly, a person who is rejected or abandoned by a romantic partner may introject their partner's negative evaluation of them and believe that they are unworthy of love or happiness.

Another function of introjection is coping with loss or separation by preserving a bond with the lost object or person. For example, a person who loses a loved one may introject their memories, traits, or values into their personality and continue to act as if they were still present. On the one hand, this can help that person maintain connection and continuity with the deceased; on the other hand, it can also prevent them from grieving properly and moving on with their life. In some cases, introjection can lead to pathological forms of identification, such as delusions or hallucinations. Introjection can also be viewed as a means of broadening your perception of the self by incorporating desirable or admired aspects of others. For example, a person who admires a celebrity may introject their style, mannerisms, or opinions into their own behavior and expression. They can then enhance their personal identity and confidence; however, it can also result in a loss of authenticity and individuality. Moreover, introjection can create unrealistic or idealized expectations that can be difficult to fulfill or sustain.

To achieve a healthy and balanced personality, you need to be aware of introjection and its effects on your perception on the self. You need to distinguish between your thoughts and feelings and those derived from others. You need to evaluate the sources and validity of the introjected material critically and reject or modify any harmful or inappropriate material. Additionally, you need to integrate positive and useful aspects of introjection into your identity while maintaining autonomy and differentiation from others. This can prove challenging when dealing with specific aspects of early-life introjected emotions. Introjected feelings can be subtle and difficult to discern. For example, my own mother's negativity and her inability to care for my needs were something I introjected at a very young age in the form of feeling inadequate or unworthy. I was never enough. But what about you?

Exercise #1

So, Who Made You?

This exercise is designed to help you recognize your attachment style and possible introjected emotions. Once you've identified them, the second part will address ways you can heal negative influences.

Part 1

Identifying

One way to determine your attachment style and introjected emotions is to use the following exercise:

1. Think of a significant person in your life, such as a parent, partner, friend, or sibling. Write down their name and your relationship with them.
2. Recall a recent, emotionally charged interaction with this person, either positive or negative. Write down what happened, how you felt, what you said, and what they said.
3. Consider how this interaction mirrors or exemplifies your attachment style with this person. Use the four categories of attachment styles: secure, anxious, avoidant, or fearful. Write down which category best describes your attachment style and why.
4. Identify any introjected emotions that you experienced during or after the interaction. Introjected emotions are emotions that you have internalized from others, such as

guilt, shame, anger, or fear. Write down which introjected emotions you felt and where they came from.
5. Evaluate how your attachment style and introjected emotions affect your relationship with this person and yourself. Write down what you would like to change or improve in your attachment style and introjected emotions, as well as the steps you can take to achieve those changes.

This exercise can provide valuable insight into your attachment style, introjected emotions, and their impact on your interpersonal dynamics as well as self-esteem. For a more comprehensive understanding of your attachment patterns and emotional regulation, you can replicate this exercise with various other individuals in your life.

Part 2

Healing

This exercise is designed to help you heal negative introjected emotions and insecure attachment styles, with the objective to practice self-compassion and positive affirmations. Self-compassion is the ability to treat yourself with kindness, understanding, and acceptance, especially when facing difficulties or failures. Positive affirmations are statements that reinforce your strengths, values, and worthiness.

To practice self-compassion and positive affirmations, you can follow these steps:

1. Identify a situation that triggers negative emotions or insecurity in you. For example, you may feel ashamed of making a mistake at work or anxious about losing your partner's love.
2. Notice how you talk to yourself about the situation. Do you use harsh, critical, or blaming words? Do you exaggerate the

negative aspects or ignore the positive ones? Do you compare yourself unfavorably to others or doubt your abilities? Write down examples of any negative self-talk you may have.
3. Imagine how you would talk to a friend in the same situation. What words of comfort, support, or encouragement would you use? How would you help them see the situation more realistically and constructively? Write down examples of positive statements you would make.
4. Replace your self-talk with the friend-talk. Use the same words and tone you would use with a friend. Acknowledge your feelings without judging them and remind yourself of your strengths and achievements. Express gratitude for what you have and hope for what you want. Do this actively; don't just think about it. Look at yourself in the mirror as you say the words out loud.
5. Repeat this exercise whenever you encounter a challenging situation or feel insecure in your relationships.

Over time, you will develop a more positive and compassionate relationship with yourself and others. You will retrain your brain to use positive self-talk anytime you're confronted with negative emotions and situations.

Final Thoughts on Who Made You

As you delve into your early life experiences that led to negative introjected emotions and insecure attachment styles, you may also confront difficult emotions that impact your daily life. This is normal and to be expected, so be gentle with yourself when this happens. Take a moment to excuse yourself from any interactions you're currently having and sit with your emotions for a moment. Tell yourself that your emotions are valid and that you want to deal with them properly. Make a commitment to yourself to delve into the depth of your experiences when the timing is right, and ensure that you follow through on this pledge. This is how you will heal, and it will be the most important thing you will ever do. It colors all of your other life experiences, so treat it with the appropriate level of respect, kindness, and self-love that you have always deserved. You didn't always get it, but now, you can give it to yourself. This is just the beginning of exploring your inner emotional landscape, so it's vital that you establish a strong foundation of self-respect and self-love. Doing so will carry you through what's to come.

Chapter 2

Exploring Within to Heal Throughout

Healing codependency is, as they say, an inside job. You have to go deep inside to discover the source of your wounds and how those scars shaped your behavior. The truth is not out there; it's *in* there. It's inside, and going to that inside place will be one of the most difficult journeys you'll ever make. It will, however, also be one of the most rewarding. To heal your codependent patterns of behavior, it is crucial to embark on an inward exploration. As you uncover the underlying origins of your thought patterns and behaviors, you can begin the process of healing those wounds and transforming your behaviors.

What Do You Truly Believe?

Back when my mother would criticize me relentlessly at a young age, I would adopt certain assumptions about myself. I started believing that I was worthless, stupid, inept, and unworthy of love. Core beliefs, which develop during childhood, significantly influence our interpersonal behaviors; for me, specifically, they contributed to my pursuit of self-love through the validation of others. They are fundamental assumptions that shape how we perceive ourselves, others, and the world. These beliefs form as a result of our experiences and interactions with family, peers, teachers, and other influential individuals. Core beliefs can be positive or negative, and they can have a profound impact on how a person thinks, feels, and behaves throughout their life.

Codependent patterns of behavior are often rooted in core beliefs formed in childhood and reinforced by dysfunctional relationships. Some common core beliefs that can produce codependent patterns of behavior include:

- I am not good enough.
- I have to please others to be loved.
- I am responsible for other people's happiness and problems.
- I have to sacrifice my needs for others.
- I have no control over my life.
- I need someone else to make me feel complete.

These core beliefs can lead to codependent behaviors, such as:

- Being overly dependent on or attached to someone else.
- Trying to fix, rescue, or save someone else from their issues.
- Neglecting or suppressing one's own needs, feelings, and desires.
- Having poor boundaries and allowing others to violate them.
- Feeling guilty, ashamed, or resentful when saying no or setting limits.
- Having low self-esteem and self-worth.
- Being afraid of rejection, abandonment, or conflict.
- Having difficulty expressing one's own opinions, preferences, or emotions.

These codependent behaviors can have negative consequences on your mental health, well-being, and relationships, and they can cause stress, anxiety, depression, anger, resentment, loneliness, isolation, and dissatisfaction. They can also prevent you from achieving goals, fulfilling your potential, and living authentically. The first step to breaking free from codependent patterns of behavior is to identify and challenge any core beliefs that underlie them. This can be done with the help of a therapist, support group, or self-help program. By changing your core beliefs, you can then change your perspective, attitude, and behaviors. You can learn to:

- Accept yourself as you are and value yourself as a person.
- Recognize and meet your own needs, feelings, and desires.
- Establish and maintain healthy boundaries with others.
- Communicate assertively and respectfully with others.
- Develop autonomy and agency over your own life.
- Seek healthy and fulfilling relationships with others.

Core beliefs are not always easy to uncover however, since they are often subconscious and automatic—which would mean that they are not easily accessible or questioned by the conscious mind. They act as filters that influence how a person perceives and interprets reality. For instance, a person with the core belief that they are incompetent and inadequate may attribute their successes to luck or external factors and their failures to their own flaws or shortcomings. They may also avoid taking risks or pursuing opportunities that could challenge their core beliefs and expose them to failure or criticism. Moreover, they may be completely unaware of these patterns. They're not consciously thinking, "I'm attributing my successes to luck and my inadequacies to my own flaws;" they're doing it automatically. It's a habit.

By acknowledging those negative core beliefs, you can establish healthier and more positive habits, ultimately leading to a complete transformation of your behavior. For example, a person who believes that they are incompetent and inadequate may learn to recognize their strengths and achievements habitually, acknowledge their limitations and areas for improvement, and accept themselves as a person capable of learning and growing. They can then see that it's not an inherent flaw in their character; their behavior is just the result of learned conditioning that they accepted as true. When you've been told enough times that you're stupid, you start believing that must be true. Once you start challenging that assumption, you will then see that you're not stupid at all. You might be ignorant or make poor decisions, but that does not equate to stupidity.

Recognizing the Problem

Recognizing our core beliefs can help us understand why we react the way we do to certain situations, and we can also then challenge the limiting or negative ones. One way to recognize our core beliefs is to identify the thoughts that pop up in our mind when we face a problem or a stressful event. These thoughts are often distorted or exaggerated and reflect our underlying beliefs. For example, if we fail a test and think, "I'm stupid and worthless," we may have a core belief that we are not good enough or that we need to be perfect. What is your inner dialogue like? Another way to recognize our core beliefs is to examine our emotional and behavioral patterns over time. If we notice that we often feel anxious, depressed, angry, or insecure, we may have some core beliefs that are causing us distress. Similarly, if we notice that we tend to avoid certain situations, people, or activities, some of our core beliefs may be holding us back from living fully. The next time you decide you don't want to go to that family gathering or dinner with your friends, ask yourself if your decision is really based on your introverted nature (nothing wrong with that) or because you think they will find you boring. If it is the latter case, it is possible that you have internalized a limiting core belief that is impeding your progress.

A third way to recognize our core beliefs is to trace them back to their origins. Core beliefs are usually formed in childhood or adolescence as a result of experiences with our family, peers, teachers, and society. They may also be influenced by our culture, religion, gender, and personality. By reflecting their development, we can gain more insight into their validity and usefulness. Recognizing our core beliefs is the first step toward changing them. Once we identify them, we can evaluate them objectively and challenge them with evidence and alternative perspectives. We can also replace them with more positive and realistic ones that can support our well-being and growth. We can then improve our self-esteem, confidence, and happiness.

Changing Your Core Beliefs

Core beliefs can be positive or negative and can be helpful or unhelpful in different situations. However, some core beliefs are rigid, distorted, or unrealistic and can cause us to suffer unnecessarily or limit our potential.

Changing core beliefs is not easy, but it is possible with consistent effort and practice. Here are some steps you can follow to identify and modify your core beliefs:

1. **Identify your core beliefs:** You can do this by paying attention to your automatic thoughts and making note of any themes or patterns that emerge. For example, if you often think, "I'm not good enough" or "I always fail," you might have a core belief of being inadequate or incompetent.
2. **Challenge your core beliefs:** You can achieve this by seeking evidence that either challenges or reinforces your core beliefs. For example, if you have a core belief of being inadequate, you can list some of your achievements or strengths that prove otherwise. You can also ask yourself questions like "Is this belief true?" "Is this belief helpful?" "Where did this belief come from?" and "What would I tell a friend who had this belief?"
3. **Replace your core beliefs.** You can achieve this by developing new core beliefs that reflect your authentic values and goals while also being realistic and adaptable. For example, instead of believing "I'm not good enough," you can replace it with "I'm worthy of respect and love" or "I can learn from my mistakes and grow." You can also use

affirmations, visualization, or other techniques to reinforce your new core beliefs.
4. **Practice your new core beliefs:** You act in ways that are consistent with your new core beliefs and noticing how they affect your emotions and behaviors. For instance, if you embrace the core belief that you are capable, you can push yourself to explore new experiences and take on additional responsibilities. You can also reward yourself for your efforts and achievements and celebrate your progress.

Changing core beliefs takes time and patience, but it can impact your well-being and happiness profoundly. By identifying, challenging, replacing, and practicing new core beliefs, you can then transform your self-image and outlook on life.

Learning to Accept Who You Really Are

Understanding and changing negative core beliefs is a big part of exploring your inner psyche, but there's another important component of this work that is vital to healing. Most codependents, such as myself, don't think of themselves as worthy—worthy of love, respect, or kindness. As proof, they point to the flaws and mistakes they've made. Usually, these are things that someone in your life has pointed out many times in the past. Learning to accept who you are is one of the most crucial aspects of personal growth and happiness. It means recognizing your strengths and weaknesses, values and beliefs, emotions and motivations, and dreams and aspirations. It also means accepting your limitations and challenges, mistakes and failures, and flaws and imperfections. Accepting who you are does not mean settling for less or giving up on yourself; it means being honest and realistic about yourself and embracing your uniqueness and diversity. It means loving yourself, no matter your flaws or mistakes you make; you love yourself just because you are worthy of love.

There are many benefits of learning to accept who you are. First, it can enhance your self-esteem and confidence by freeing you from the habit of comparing yourself to others or seeking external validation. You can appreciate your worth and potential and celebrate your achievements and progress. Second, it can improve your mental health and well-being since you are reducing stress and anxiety. You are also coping better with challenges and setbacks and cultivating more positive emotions. Additionally, you can cultivate a mindset that is more balanced and adaptable, steering clear of negative thoughts and behaviors such as self-criticism, perfectionism, and procrastination. Third, it can enhance your relationships with others by communicating more authentically and respectfully, expressing your needs and boundaries more clearly, and empathizing more deeply with others. Furthermore, you have the ability to draw in individuals who are supportive and compatible, foster healthier relationships, and approach conflict resolution more constructively.

Learning to accept who you are is not always easy or straightforward, however. It requires courage and commitment, as well as patience and compassion. It is a lifelong process that involves constant reflection, feedback, experimentation, and adaptation. Here are some tips to help you learn to accept who you are:

- **Identify your core values and beliefs:** These principles will serve as the guiding force behind your decisions and actions, reflecting the utmost importance of what truly matters to you in life. They can be based on your personal experiences, cultural background, spiritual beliefs, or moral convictions. Knowing your core values and beliefs can help you align your actions with your purpose and thus live more authentically and meaningfully. It helps you to live with integrity.

- **Recognize your strengths and weaknesses:** These are the qualities that make you good or bad at certain tasks or situations. They can be related to your skills, talents, knowledge, personality traits, or habits. Understanding your strengths and weaknesses can aid in leveraging your assets, improving areas for growth, and selecting goals and activities aligned with your abilities and interests. This is all in good sentiment, but acknowledging weaknesses can be difficult because it can be hard to admit your flaws. For example, I wish I could sing, but one of my weaknesses is that I don't have a good voice. That doesn't make me a bad person or that I can't express myself musically; it just means that I shouldn't quit my day job for a singing career—which is entirely okay! I can acknowledge that weakness and focus my efforts, including my musical expression, elsewhere.
- **Acknowledge your emotions and motivations:** These are the feelings that influence one's mood and behavior and the reasons that drive you to do or avoid something. They can be based on your needs, desires, fears, hopes, or expectations. Recognizing your emotions and motivations helps you better manage your impulses and reactions while also helping you understand what brings you happiness or unhappiness. For example, as a codependent, you might recognize that you have a tendency to feel unhappy unless you are helping serve someone else's needs. When you can acknowledge that motivation and the emotions behind it, you can then find ways to help others without neglecting your own needs. Assisting others isn't the bad part of codependency. It is when your self-worth becomes reliant on the compulsion to help others that a positive trait can turn into a vulnerability. Recognizing that can be the key to freeing yourself.
- **Explore your dreams and aspirations:** These are the visions that inspire you to pursue something bigger or better in life. They can be related to your career, education, family,

health, hobbies, or social causes. Recognizing your dreams and aspirations can help you set meaningful goals and plan realistic strategies to achieve them. Most codependents put aside their dreams and aspirations in favor of fostering someone else's. But that doesn't serve you, and in the end, it doesn't serve them. To be of genuine service to others, you first have to realize your own dreams and work toward making them your reality.

- **Accept your limitations and challenges:** These are the factors that may hinder or prevent you from doing or reaching a goal. They can be related to your physical conditions, mental health issues, financial constraints, social barriers, or environmental obstacles. Accepting your limitations and challenges does not mean giving up on or ignoring them; it means being aware of them and finding ways to overcome or adapt to them. For example, you might have to accept that you don't have the money to get a specific degree, but that doesn't mean you can't learn what you need to know for your dream job. You can still approach getting that dream job from a different perspective.

- **Accept your mistakes and failures:** These are the outcomes that do not meet your expectations or standards. They can be related to your performance, judgment, behavior, or communication. Accepting your mistakes and failures does not mean justifying them or repeating them. It means learning from them and moving on from them. When you fail, learning from it is key to both doing better in the future and moving beyond the limitations that failure might create. Engaging in sincere introspection is necessary to evaluate your failures thoroughly. When you embrace this process, then will you discover the potential that lies within them. For instance, consider a situation where you undertook a project but didn't achieve the desired outcome. What did you learn from that experience, and how can it help you in the future?

Maybe you learned about what not to do as much as you learned what you should do.
- **Accept your flaws and imperfections:** These are the aspects of yourself that you dislike or wish to change. They can be related to your appearance, personality, attitudes, or preferences. Accepting your flaws and imperfections means loving yourself despite them and embracing them as a part of the whole "you." At this stage, many people make the mistake of allowing these flaws to shape their identity. Your flaws don't define you, and they don't invalidate your inherent worth as a person. You might be a bit overweight, but that doesn't make you a bad person. You might have a big nose, but that doesn't mean you're not attractive. You might want to lose weight or get a nose job, and that's fine because that doesn't define you, either. Your self-worth is something you possess, no matter your imperfections.

Embarking on the path of self-acceptance is a fulfilling voyage that can greatly enrich your life. It nurtures personal growth, propels you toward your aspirations, and enhances your connections with others. Moreover, it empowers you to make a positive impact on the world by sharing your unique gifts, talents, and passions. Remember that you are unique, valuable, and worthy of respect, love, and happiness. You are enough just as you are.

Exercise #2

Finding and Challenging Your Core Beliefs

Core beliefs are sneaky. They hide within our psyche and manipulate our behavior. Negative beliefs are like parasites, latching onto our mindset and leading us astray from our true potential and happiness. But you can expose and challenge those core beliefs, and this is another two-part exercise to do that. The first step will be exposing your core beliefs.

Part 1

Identifying Your Core Beliefs

One way to identify your core beliefs is to practice a meditation exercise that involves self-inquiry and reflection:

1. Find a comfortable and quiet place where you can sit or lie down without distractions. Close your eyes and take 10 deep breaths to relax your body and mind. These breaths should expand both your chest and your stomach.
2. Bring your attention to your heart center: the area in the middle of your chest. Imagine a warm and gentle light in your heart radiating love and compassion. Feel this light expanding and filling your whole being with peace and joy.
3. Ask yourself: What do I believe about myself? What do I believe about others? What do I believe about the world? Listen to the answers that come up in your mind without judging or rejecting them. Just observe them as they are.
4. For each answer, ask yourself: Is this belief true? How do I know it is true? What evidence do I have to support it? How does this belief make me feel? How does this belief affect my actions and decisions? Be honest with and curious about yourself.
5. If you find a belief that is negative, unhelpful, or distorted, ask yourself: Where did this belief come from? When did I learn it? Who taught it to me? How did it serve me in the past? How is it limiting me now? What would happen if I let go of this belief?
6. If you find a belief that is positive, helpful, or accurate, ask yourself: How can I strengthen this belief? How can I use it to empower myself and others? How can I express it in my life? How can I celebrate it?
7. Once you have explored your core beliefs, thank yourself for doing this exercise and acknowledge your courage and

willingness to grow. Redirect your focus to the center of your heart and reconnect with the radiant light residing within. Send some of this light to yourself and anyone or anything you wish to bless. Open your eyes and return to consciousness.

Part 2

Changing Your Core Beliefs

One exercise for challenging and changing negative core beliefs is to use a cognitive restructuring technique called Socratic questioning. Socratic questioning is a method of asking open-ended questions to help you examine your thoughts and beliefs more critically and logically. The goal is to identify and challenge any distortions, errors, or irrationalities in your thinking that may be causing you emotional distress or interfering with your goals.

To use Socratic questioning, you can follow these steps:

1. Identify a negative core belief that you want to change. For example, "I am worthless."
2. Write down any evidence that would support this belief. For example, "I failed an exam," "I got rejected by someone I liked," or "I don't have many friends."
3. Now, write down evidence that contradicts this belief. For example, "I passed other exams before," "There are people who care about me," "I have qualities that I like about myself."
4. Ask yourself questions that challenge the validity, accuracy, and usefulness of your belief. For example, "Is this belief based on facts or feelings?" "Is this belief always true or are there exceptions?" "How does this belief help or hurt me?" and "What would I tell a friend who had this belief?"
5. Based on your answers, come up with a more balanced and realistic alternative belief that takes into account both the

positive and negative aspects of yourself and your situation. For example, "I am not worthless; I have strengths and weaknesses like everyone else."
6. Repeat this exercise whenever you become aware of negative core beliefs and wish to replace them with more positive ones through consistent practice.
7. Write down your list of alternative beliefs; every time you notice your negative self-talk kick in, pull out your list and replace that negative belief with a positive alternative.

Final Thoughts on Core Beliefs

The core beliefs that you've accepted as true often form in an instant. As a child, you pick up offhand comments made by those you love and respect, and you make a judgment about yourself as a result of those comments. At times, such beliefs stem from abusive experiences by a caretaker who, despite intending to act in your best interest, may have been too emotionally wounded to fulfill the role of a nurturing parent. But the core beliefs we adopt are not who we truly are. We are so much more than that, and by identifying and changing your core beliefs, you are acknowledging that fact. You are acknowledging that not only are you not worthless, stupid, unkind, or insensitive; rather, you are beautiful, and you have the capacity to change. By embarking on this journey of healing, you have already demonstrated your remarkable courage. That alone shows you're far more than what you identified with as a frightened and impressionable child. To truly heal those core beliefs, it is crucial to identify the emotional triggers stemming from the wounds we experienced during our early years. That's what the next chapter will explore.

Chapter 3

Identifying Emotional Triggers and Wounds

All of us walk this world wounded. Even those with the brightest of childhoods have had some sort of wound that they carry with them into their adult lives. Although painful when experienced, these wounds serve as profound opportunities for growth. They form part of who we are, and if we live to adulthood, we are, above all else, survivors. That's an incredible and empowering way to look at the wounds you received, no matter how awful they were at the start. Somehow you survived, and doesn't that make you an extraordinary person? I think it does, and when you learn to recognize that too, you can then defuse your triggers and heal those wounds. You can become the superhero you have always wanted to become. You can replace outdated behaviors with healthier coping mechanisms that foster personal growth. The process begins with understanding what the emotional triggers represent and identifying yours.

What Triggers You?

Emotional triggers are stimuli that evoke strong emotional reactions in us like anger, fear, sadness, or joy. They can be external, such as words, actions, or events, or internal, such as memories, thoughts, or feelings. Emotional triggers stem from intense, traumatic, or recurring past experiences and associations. They can affect our behavior in various ways, depending on how we cope with them.

Some examples of emotional triggers include:

- Hearing a song that reminds us of a happy or painful memory.
- Seeing a familiar face of someone who hurt or helped us.
- Smelling a scent that brings back a memory of a place or person.
- Feeling a physical sensation tied to an emotion, such as a tight chest or a warm hug.
- Reading or watching something that resonates with our values or beliefs.

When triggered, we may subconsciously react without awareness of the underlying cause. This can lead to impulsive, irrational, harmful, or otherwise inappropriate behavior. For example, we may lash out at someone who says something that reminds us of a past insult, or we may avoid a situation that makes us feel anxious or vulnerable. The alternative is that we respond consciously and intentionally by recognizing and regulating our emotions and choosing how to act accordingly. This can lead to adaptive, rational, and more appropriate behavior that may benefit ourselves or others. For example, we may use humor to diffuse a tense situation or seek support from someone who understands us. Emotional triggers can be an opportunity for growth and healing if we learn how to identify and cope with them effectively. Becoming more aware of our emotional triggers and their origins enhances our self-understanding and empathy toward others. Additionally, as we develop healthy coping skills and strategies to manage these triggers, we can minimize their negative effects and foster greater emotional resilience and well-being.

Before we go further, let's take a look at the four levels of emotional reactions that we typically have.

The Four Levels of Emotional Reactions

The four levels of emotional reactions are physiological arousal, cognitive appraisal, subjective experience, and behavioral response. These four levels form a cycle of emotion, and understanding each one can help us better recognize our own emotional reactions and the emotions of others.

1. Physiological Arousal
2. Cognitive Appraisal
3. Subjective Experience
4. Behavioral Response

The first level is that of physiological arousal, which is the physical response we experience when our body reacts to a particular emotion. This could include increased heart rate, and increased breathing, among other physical reactions.

The second level is cognitive appraisal, which is how we interpret our emotions. We consider the context of the emotion and decide whether it's positive or negative. We may also assign a label to the emotion, such as "happy" or "sad."

The third level is subjective experience, which is how we feel the emotion. It encompasses the emotional aspect of our reaction, which we can often articulate using words like "joy" or "anger."

The fourth level is behavioral response, which is how we act on the emotion. This could include verbal or physical reactions, such as shouting or hugging. Understanding these four levels of emotional reactions can enhance our comprehension of both our own emotions and the emotional responses of others. It also aids in improving our emotional management by teaching us to foster self-awareness of our feelings and enabling us to respond more appropriately to different situations.

Four More Levels

According to psychologist Robert Plutchik, emotions can further be categorized into four more levels: primary, secondary, tertiary, and quaternary. Let's explore how these levels reflect different emotional triggers and how they can affect our behavior and well-being.

1. **Primary Emotions:** Primary emotions are the most basic and instinctive ones, such as joy, sadness, anger, fear, surprise, and disgust. They are triggered by events that directly impact our survival, such as threats, losses, or rewards. Primary emotions are universal and innate, meaning that they are shared by all humans and animals, and they do not depend on learning or culture.
2. **Secondary Emotions:** Secondary emotions are more complex and nuanced, examples being guilt, shame, pride, envy, jealousy, and gratitude. They are triggered by events with an indirect impact on our survival, such as social interactions, moral judgments, or self-evaluation. Secondary emotions are influenced by learning and culture, meaning that they vary across individuals and groups and depend primarily on social norms and values.
3. **Tertiary Emotions:** Tertiary emotions are even more complex and subtle than secondary emotions. They include emotions like awe, wonder, curiosity, boredom, anticipation, and disappointment and are triggered by events with no immediate impact on our survival; rather, they have to do with our cognitive and aesthetic interests. Tertiary emotions are driven by learning and culture, meaning they depend on our knowledge and preferences while reflecting our goals and motivations.
4. **Quaternary Emotions:** Quaternary emotions are the most complex and refined of the four types and include emotions

such as compassion, empathy, sympathy, love, hate, and contempt. They are triggered by events that involve other people's emotions or perspectives. Quaternary emotions are based on learning and culture, meaning they require a high level of cognitive and social skills and express our moral and ethical values.

These levels reflect different aspects of our human nature and experience. Understanding them can help us regulate our emotions better and improve our relationship with ourselves and others.

The Importance of Identifying and Defusing Emotional Triggers

I remember that on one of my very first dates, my date made a very casual remark about the dress I was wearing. It wasn't intended as an insult, and in fact, he meant it as a compliment, but the way he said it triggered intense shame in me. I recall experiencing an overwhelming surge of shame and self-blame, accompanied by a flood of emotions and thoughts. I was fully triggered. Needless to say, the date didn't last very long, but my shame did. I remember trying so hard to understand why I had felt the way I did. I didn't remember a specific incident in my past, and I wasn't consciously aware of any particular wound related to that. My dress wasn't risque; it just looked nice on me. That was my intention for the date, yet, inexplicably, I emerged from the experience feeling dirty. It took me a considerable amount of time to comprehend the origin of those unsettling feelings and the underlying reason for believing that I had let someone down in some way. This is how an emotional trigger sneaks into our lived experiences. Unrelated actions or circumstances can unexpectedly evoke a strong response, even if they have no direct connection to the original source of your emotional trigger. A passing comment, a scent, a color, a taste, or various other stimuli may have the power to elicit such intense reactions. Emotional triggers stem from past experiences, including trauma, abuse, neglect, or loss, which have imprinted lasting impressions on our psyche. Encountering a trigger can lead to disproportionate or harmful reactions that extend beyond the present situation, impacting both ourselves and others. For example, we may lash out at our partner for being late because it reminds us of a time when we felt abandoned by someone we loved. Or, as in my case, we may shame ourselves ruthlessly due to our negative core beliefs.

Identifying and defusing emotional triggers is becoming more aware of our feelings and reactions and learning to cope with them healthily. Recognizing triggers involves identifying physical sensations, thoughts, or behaviors, understanding their source in memories, beliefs, or needs, and finding soothing and calming techniques like breathing exercises, meditation, or self-compassion. By doing this, we can reduce the intensity and frequency of our emotional reactions and prevent them from escalating into conflicts or crises.

Healing the wounds that created these triggers involves a thorough and ongoing process of addressing the underlying issues that have caused us pain and distress. It involves exploring our past experiences and how they have shaped us, acknowledging and expressing our emotions and needs, challenging and changing our negative beliefs and patterns, and seeking support and guidance from others who can help us heal. By doing this, we can gradually heal our wounds and develop a more positive and resilient sense of self.

How Can Toxic People Use Emotional Triggers to Control Us?

Toxic people are those who manipulate, abuse, or harm others for their own benefit. Narcissists are an example of a toxic personality type. They often use our emotional triggers to control us and make us feel guilty, ashamed, or angry. Because emotional triggers evoke strong reactions in us, toxic people are able to easily utilize them to gain control and manipulate others. Toxic people, like my mother, spend the early stages of a relationship getting to know you in order to recognize your emotional triggers. Then, they use manipulation techniques to trigger you. Most people use this kind of manipulation without realizing they're doing it. They may have learned it from their parents or experiences, and it worked for them. But some people, like psychopaths and narcissists, will use these techniques consciously, or at least semi-consciously. They purposefully trigger you so they can then manipulate you.

One way that toxic people can use our emotional triggers is by gaslighting. This was a favorite tactic of my mother; she loved to make me question my reality. If I had a need, I was selfish, and if I wanted to do something that any young kid would want to do, I was lazy. That's what gaslighting is; it's a form of psychological abuse where the abuser makes the victim doubt their memory or perception. For example, a toxic partner may deny that they cheated on their spouse, even when there is clear evidence of their infidelity. They may even accuse their spouse of being paranoid, crazy, or insecure. They may also twist the facts or lie to make their spouse feel confused or guilty. By doing this, they are using the spouse's emotional trigger of insecurity or betrayal to make them question their sanity and judgment. My narcissistic ex-husband used this tactic frequently and was very skilled at twisting any argument we had into being my fault. My own codependency played a role in this abuse too. I felt like I needed him, and I desperately wanted to please him—and I questioned whether I was being unreasonable. He was so certain that I was, and since I was isolated from my friends and family members, I had no one to turn to for another perspective. When someone is successful at this technique, their victim will believe they have to rely on the toxic individual for a proper interpretation of reality.

Another way that toxic people can use our emotional triggers to control us is by projecting. Projecting is a defense mechanism where the person attributes their own negative feelings or traits onto someone else. For example, a toxic boss may blame their employees for their own mistakes or failures. They may criticize their employees for being lazy, incompetent, or dishonest and may also accuse them of having ulterior motives or hidden agendas. By doing this, they are using the employees' emotional triggers of fear or anxiety to make them feel inferior or unworthy. Narcissists often accuse others of being narcissistic, particularly when they can steal the spotlight away from the narcissist. This is a classic example of projecting; they are projecting their own toxic traits onto their victims. Oftentimes, the victims are so confused that they begin to believe the projection.

A third way that toxic people can use our emotional triggers is for triangulating. Triangulating is a manipulation tactic where the person creates conflict or drama between two or more people. For example, they may gossip about one friend to another, spreading rumors, lies, or secrets that could cause mistrust or jealousy between those two friends. They may also play the victim or hero in different situations to gain sympathy or admiration from others. By doing this, they are using the friends' emotional triggers of anger or envy to make them fight with each other. Narcissists often use triangulation to create an atmosphere of mistrust between family members. They don't want their victims to be close enough to anyone else in the family to figure out what they're doing. In this way, you believe you don't have anyone you can turn to for another point of view.

Toxic individuals have the ability to inflict significant harm by exploiting our emotional triggers, and manipulating us psychologically. Therefore, it is crucial to identify and neutralize our own triggers, ensuring that they cannot be weaponized against us by anyone. The truth is that you should be able to be vulnerable with the person you love. You should be able to show them your wounds and trust that they won't use them against you. But so many people have damaged themselves, and that person could use what they learned about you to manipulate and further abuse you. When you defuse that trigger and heal that old wound, you take away that weapon. You take back control over your own emotional responses, and you can be vulnerable without exposing yourself to manipulation and abuse.

We tend to mistake our stories for our identity, but they are not one and the same. Your story is simply something that happened to you; it's not who you are. Who you are is so much more profound than any one story from your life. It's common to get caught up in the narratives our minds create, which can lead us to be carried away by our emotions. When you realize that the story is just that: a story, then can you let it go. You can let it be a part of your life without making it a part of your identity. Then you can really see the gifts that the story has given you and how it has made you stronger.

Codependency and Emotional Triggers

Codependent people are especially vulnerable to emotional triggers because they have learned to suppress their l needs and feelings to please others. Codependency is a dysfunctional relationship pattern that often develops in childhood when caregivers are emotionally unavailable, abusive, or neglectful. Codependent people grow up feeling insecure, unworthy, and afraid of abandonment. They seek validation and self-worth from external sources, such as their partners, friends, or family members, and develop patterns of behavior that allow them to love themselves through other people's love for them. In my own situation, I wanted to please the people in my life so they would love me, and when they loved me for all I was doing for them, I was, in that sense, loving myself. But to get that sensation, I put everyone else's needs above my own, neglecting my own needs and desires. I suppressed what I wanted because I so desperately needed the other person to love me and see my worth. My childhood experiences left me with very low self-esteem. It didn't feel like I was enough, but if I could just do enough for other people, and they loved me for that, then I could feel worthy of love. You can probably see how this set me up for emotional abuse and control.

Emotional triggers can be used to manipulate codependent people by exploiting their fears and insecurities. For example, someone may accuse their codependent partner of being selfish or too sensitive when they express their opinions or desires. This can trigger guilt, shame, and self-doubt in the codependent person, who may then apologize and comply with their partner's wishes. This often happened with my narcissistic ex. Alternatively, the individual may use threats of leaving or ignoring their codependent partner as a means to discourage the partner from establishing boundaries or asserting their needs. This can trigger anxiety, panic, and abandonment in the codependent person, who may then beg for forgiveness and cling to the partner.

It's easy for some toxic people to identify your weaknesses. They may recognize that you fear abandonment, perhaps because you told them in the earlier idealization stage of your relationship. Narcissists, for example, will use that early period to be as charming as they can possibly be. It is believed that many romantic partners of narcissists meet their "soulmates" during this early stage. Narcissists are extremely charming at this point in the relationship, but they can't maintain that facade for long. That's why they learn everything they can about you in that early stage. Even when they seem ever so charming, they are actually gathering ammunition to use against you. They learn about your vulnerabilities, old wounds, and emotional triggers. Then, they can discern how to use them against you.

Emotional manipulation can have harmful effects on codependent people's mental and physical health. It can erode their self-esteem, identity, and autonomy. It can also cause them to experience chronic stress, depression, anxiety, and other psychological problems. Moreover, emotional manipulation can prevent codependent people from developing healthy and interdependent relationships with others.

After leaving my narcissistic ex, I was extremely depressed. I experienced deep feelings of loneliness and a lack of love. What's worse, I believed that I didn't deserve love. This is codependency. The toxic person wants someone with this kind of behavioral pattern to feel this exactly. Had I not recognized that something was wrong with me and pursued a journey of healing, I might have gone running back to my narcissistic ex, pleading for his forgiveness. Many codependent people do just that—and there were certainly times in my life when I had reacted very similarly. But you can break free of that kind of control. Codependent people can overcome emotional manipulation by becoming aware of their triggers and how those triggers affect behavior. They can also learn to recognize the signs of manipulation and set boundaries with their partners. So how can you recognize and defuse your emotional triggers? Let's take a look.

Exercise #3

Trigger Warning

Recognizing, defusing, and healing emotional triggers consists of two essential components. The first part revolves around identifying and diffusing the triggers themselves. The second part focuses on actively addressing and healing the original wound that gave rise to the trigger.

Part 1

Identifying Your Triggers

Identifying our emotional triggers can help us understand ourselves better and cope with difficult emotions more effectively. Here are the steps to take when identifying your emotional triggers:

1. **Reflect on your past experiences:** When you have a quiet moment where you can reflect without interruption, engage in uninterrupted reflection. Find a peaceful space, sit quietly, and delve into moments when you experienced intense emotions, be it positive or negative. It can be something recent or something that happened a long time ago.
2. **Tell the story:** What was the situation? Who was involved? What did you say or do? How did you feel afterward? Recall as many details as possible and write them down in a journal.
3. **Look for patterns:** After reflecting on several situations where you had a strong emotional response over the course of a week or two, review your journal entries and see if you can find any common triggering themes. For example, you might notice that you tend to feel angry when someone criticizes you, or maybe you feel happy when you receive praise or appreciation. You might also notice that certain people, places, or topics tend to trigger your emotions more often than others.
4. **Understand the underlying causes:** Once you have identified those patterns and recognized your emotional triggers, take the opportunity to delve deeper into understanding why they have such a significant impact on you. What's the story you tell yourself when triggered? What beliefs, values, or expectations do you have that make you react strongly to certain situations? For example, if you feel angry when someone criticizes you, it might be because you believe you need to be perfect or that you are not good

enough. If you feel happy when you receive praise or appreciation, it might be because you value recognition or approval from others.

5. **Learn to manage your emotions:** Knowing your emotional triggers can help you prepare for and deal with them more effectively. You can use various strategies to cope with your emotions, such as breathing exercises, relaxation techniques, positive affirmations, cognitive restructuring, or seeking support from others. You can also try to avoid or minimize exposure to your emotional triggers, if possible and appropriate. For example, if you know that a certain person or topic tends to make you angry, you can try to limit your contact with them or change the subject. Try this the next time you feel triggered:

- Take 10 deep breaths before responding to the situation. Breathe into both your belly and chest.
- After calming yourself with breathing, repeat an appropriate affirmation. For example, if you feel bad because someone criticized you, try repeating the following affirmation: *I am not my mistake. Like everyone, I am human, and I make mistakes, and I can learn from them. My value as a person is independent of any mistakes I make.*
- Utilize your positive self-talk from Chapter 2. For example, if you did something wrong and your first thought is, "I'm so stupid," stop and use your positive alternative. It might be something like, "I'm glad I made that mistake because now I have learned something new."

Part 2

Healing Those Old Wounds

Identifying your triggers is just the first part of dealing with them. The next step is identifying and healing the old wound that created them. Here's one method you can use to do that.

1. **Reengage with the story:** Sit again in a quiet place where you won't be interrupted. Bring to mind a time when you felt strongly triggered. Replay that situation until you can once again feel the emotions associated with the trigger.
2. **Remember the first time:** Once you're fully engaged with the emotion associated with your trigger, try to remember the first time you felt that way. This may require revisiting events from your distant past, as they are often deeply ingrained in our memories and can be readily recalled.
3. **Look at the situation with different eyes:** When this wound happened, you were someone very different from the person you've become. You were probably just a child and didn't know how to respond to the situation. View the situation again through your adult eyes. Can you see your little self trying to cope? Can you have compassion and empathy for that child? How should they have been treated?

    Now that you are aware of the harm that was inflicted, what actions or steps would you take moving forward? How would you comfort them? Do it now the way it should have been done then.
4. **See the other side:** Turn your attention and insight to the other people in that situation. Can you see the person or people who made you feel bad about yourself? Can you see them through compassionate eyes? Can you see a mother struggling to raise a child by herself or dealing with her own psychological damage? Can you envision a father who grew up in an abusive household and lacks knowledge of effective parenting techniques due to his upbringing? Can you see the damage those people endured in their lives that made them treat you the way they did? For example, in my mother's case, she was dealing with a lot of loss herself. She was also trying to salvage her family in a very dangerous part of the world during an uncertain political time. As I reflect on the instances when she caused me harm, I can see her own

desperation and pain. Although that doesn't excuse what she did—that's not the point—it does help me understand it, and with understanding comes healing.

5. **See the gift:** It's time to see the gift that situation brought you. You survived, so there's a gift there. As a child, you used whatever tactics you could to deal with your pain, and it worked because you survived. Those tactics may not serve you anymore, but they got you through that situation. While my mother encouraged my codependency by expecting me to be a caretaker in the family, in doing so, I became more resilient. I learned how to take care of other people. Granted, I put aside my own needs in doing so, but I still learned some valuable insights that I can still use, even though I now prioritize myself. I learned how to be a good caretaker—that's a valuable skill.

6. **Let the story go:** Now that you've relived this experience, you can finally let the story go. You can let it be just what it was: something that happened to you a long time ago. It no longer defines you; it's just an incident that happened in your life. Thank your little self for being so brave, bless your abuser with compassion, and let the story become just another scene in the movie that is your life.

Final Thoughts on What Triggers You

Emotional triggers and the underlying wounds that created them are ammunition that toxic people can use to control and manipulate us. For codependents, those triggers are often associated with wounds that instill worthlessness and hopelessness. We were made to believe our value was based solely on what we could do for others. The truth is that your value is inherent in your very existence. You bring light to the world and people you love, and now, you can bring it to yourself. It's time to give yourself what you should have received so many years ago. It's time to be the parent you didn't have. You can't change the past, but you can be a kind, loving, giving, and supportive caretaker to yourself going forward. You have the power to heal the child within you who is still carrying the wounds of those past traumas. Let's explore how you can go about doing just that.

Chapter 4

What Your Inner Child Needs

Inside every one of us is the child we once were. There's a little you who endured the wounds of childhood and helped you to survive some very difficult times. Everyone has experienced some kind of trauma in childhood that left scars. Our inner child retains those scars, and sometimes, that little you needs help to overcome those consequences.

The problem is that you can't go back. That's what most people who have suffered childhood trauma, particularly codependent people, are trying to do when they form adult relationships. They're trying to relive those old relationships and make them come out right this time. But that's no longer a possibility. What happened in your childhood is over and done with. Even if the people who abused you acknowledged their abusive behavior and apologized, it wouldn't heal your inner child. The damage is done, but that doesn't mean it can't be healed. You, and only you, hold the key to doing that work, however. You can heal your inner child by being the parent or friend they didn't have the first time around. That's what your inner child needs. They don't need your abusive mother, father, or whoever hurt you in your life to accept and love them; they need you to accept and love them. But before you can do that, you need to understand a little more about who your inner child really is and what they mean to you now, as an adult.

What is the Concept of the Inner Child?

The concept of the inner child refers to the psychological idea that within us exists a part of our personality that retains the qualities and characteristics of our childhood self. The inner child is often associated with creativity, spontaneity, curiosity, playfulness, and emotional expression. However, the inner child can also carry the wounds, traumas, and negative beliefs that we experienced as children. These can affect our adult behavior, relationships, and well-being.

According to some psychotherapists, such as John Bradshaw, Eric Berne, and Alice Miller, healing the inner child is an essential step in overcoming emotional problems and achieving personal growth. They suggest that by reconnecting with our inner child, we can access the positive qualities that we may have lost or suppressed while also healing the pain from our past. Some benefits of healing the inner child include:

- Increased self-esteem and self-acceptance
- Reduced anxiety and depression
- Enhanced creativity and joy
- Improved communication and intimacy
- Greater resilience and coping skills

Without healing your inner child, you may continue to live through old patterns of behavior. You might also find it difficult to overcome your struggles due to using unhelpful coping strategies.

How Does Our Inner Child Affect Our Behavior?

Our inner child is the part of us that retains the memories, emotions, and beliefs we formed in our early years. It is the source of our creativity, joy, and curiosity, but it is also of our fears, insecurities, and wounds. Our inner child plays a significant role in shaping our behavior, influencing us both positively and negatively. One of the main ways that our inner child affects our behavior is through our relationships with others. Our inner child shapes our attachment style and what we expect from others, which is how we relate to the latter emotionally. Depending on our childhood experiences, we may develop a secure, anxious, avoidant, or disorganized attachment style.

A secure attachment style means we trust others, feel comfortable with intimacy and independence, and have a positive view of ourselves and others. An anxious attachment style means we crave closeness and approval from others, are afraid of abandonment and rejection, and view ourselves and others negatively. An avoidant attachment style means we value independence and autonomy over intimacy and connection, avoid emotional involvement and commitment, and have a negative view of others while having a positive view of ourselves. A disorganized attachment style means that we have contradictory and inconsistent behaviors and expectations in relationships, experience confusion and fear around intimacy and trust, and view ourselves and others negatively.

Our attachment style affects how we communicate, express our needs and emotions, handle conflicts, and support our partners. For example, someone with an anxious attachment style may be clingy, needy, jealous, or controlling in a relationship, whereas someone with an avoidant attachment style may be distant, aloof, dismissive, or emotionally unavailable. Someone with a secure attachment style may be able to balance their own needs and emotions with those of their partner, whereas someone with a disorganized attachment style may have difficulty regulating their emotions and maintaining a stable relationship.

Another way that our inner child affects our behavior is through our self-esteem. Our self-esteem, which encompasses how we perceive our own value and assess our worthiness, is strongly influenced by the messages we received from our parents or caregivers during our childhood. If we received unconditional love, acceptance, praise, and encouragement from our parents or caregivers, we are more likely to develop healthy self-esteem. If we received criticism, rejection, neglect, or abuse from our parents or caregivers, we are more likely to develop low self-esteem. Our self-esteem affects how we perceive ourselves and behave in different situations. For example, someone with a healthy self-esteem may have confidence in their abilities and potential, take risks and challenges positively, accept compliments graciously, and cope with failures constructively. Someone with a low self-esteem may doubt their abilities and potential, avoid risks and challenges, reject compliments defensively, and dwell on failures.

A third way that our inner child affects our behavior is through our coping strategies. Our coping strategies refer to the methods we employ to navigate and manage stressors and challenges in life, and these strategies are shaped by the coping skills we learned from our parents or caregivers during our formative years. If we learned healthy coping skills from our parents or caregivers, we may develop more adaptive coping strategies. If we learned unhealthy coping skills, we may develop maladaptive coping strategies. Adaptive coping strategies help us reduce stress, resolve problems, and enhance well-being; on the other hand, maladaptive coping strategies increase stress, cause us to avoid problems, and impair our well-being. Some examples of adaptive coping strategies include seeking social support, practicing relaxation techniques, engaging in hobbies or interests, and expressing emotions appropriately. Examples of maladaptive coping strategies include isolating oneself, substance abuse or addictive behaviors, suppressing or denying emotions, and blaming yourself or others. Our coping strategies play a significant role in determining our responses to difficulties and our level of resilience in overcoming them. For instance, individuals with adaptive coping strategies often approach challenges with optimism and resourcefulness, enabling them to navigate difficulties effectively. Conversely, those with maladaptive coping strategies may feel overwhelmed by challenges, leading to pessimism and helplessness.

Our inner child influences our relationships, our self-esteem, and our coping strategies. By becoming aware of and healing our inner child, we can improve our behavior. We have the capacity to develop and embrace more effective coping strategies that empower us to navigate life's challenges. By enhancing our self-esteem and acknowledging our intrinsic worth, we can forge healthier connections with our loved ones and realize that our self-love is not contingent upon external validation. Nurturing self-compassion and self-love enables us to extend compassion and love to others as well. Those are the benefits of healing your inner child, but how do you go about doing that?

Healing Your Inner Child

There are many directions we can take to heal our inner child, depending on our needs and preferences. Some common methods include:

1. **Inner child work:** This is identifying, acknowledging, and communicating with the inner child through techniques such as journaling, meditation, visualization, art therapy, or role-playing. The goal is to understand the inner child's needs, feelings, and desires and provide them with the love, support, and validation they may have lacked in childhood. With this work, you are building your inner child a new home to live in.
2. **Reparenting:** This is a form of self-care that involves treating yourself like a loving and nurturing parent would treat a child. This means providing yourself with physical,

emotional, mental, and spiritual nourishment, such as healthy food, rest, exercise, comfort, affirmation, guidance, and discipline. The aim is to develop a positive and compassionate relationship with yourself and correct negative messages you may have internalized from your parents or caregivers.
3. **Therapy:** This is a professional intervention that can help you explore and resolve issues that stemmed from your childhood experiences. A therapist can help you identify and challenge the dysfunctional patterns you may have learned from your family, such as codependency, abuse, neglect, or abandonment. A therapist can also help you process and release any emotions you may have repressed or denied.

Healing the inner child is not necessarily a quick or easy process. It requires courage, patience, and commitment. However, it can also be rewarding and transformative. By healing the inner child, you can reclaim your true self and live a more authentic and fulfilling life.

Building a New Home for Your Inner Child

The journey of healing and growth involves constructing a renewed inner core for your inner child, enabling you to transcend past wounds and embrace your true and authentic self. Your inner child is the part of you that holds your childhood memories, emotions, and needs, both positive and negative. Sometimes, your inner child may feel hurt, scared, angry, or ashamed due to your memories and experiences. This can affect how you relate to yourself and others in the present.

To build a new inner core for your inner child, you need to acknowledge, validate, and soothe your inner child's feelings, as well as challenge and change any limiting beliefs or fears that hold you back. Here are some basic steps to help you accomplish this:

1. **Acknowledge your inner child:** Recognize that you have an inner child who needs your attention and care. You can do this by closing your eyes and imagining yourself as a child at different ages. Notice how you look, what you wear, how you feel, and what you need. What do you see when you look back on your life at different stages?
2. **Validate your inner child's feelings:** Listen to what your inner child is telling you through your emotions, sensations, thoughts, and behaviors. Don't judge, criticize, or dismiss their feelings; instead, empathize with and reassure them that they are normal, natural, and understandable. Your inner child is screaming out for your attention—don't push them away. Rather than dismissing them, lend an ear and listen to their messages. They yearn to express their needs: the unmet desires from long ago that still resonate within you.
3. **Soothe your inner child:** Offer comfort and support to your inner child when they are in distress. You can do this by hugging yourself, rocking yourself, breathing deeply, meditating, playing soothing music, or doing anything else that makes you feel calm and safe. You are the safe home for your inner child; you just need to help them recognize and know that you are a safe haven in a storm. Let them know that you will always be there for yourself and on your side.
4. **Challenge your inner child's beliefs and fears:** Identify any negative or limiting beliefs or fears that your inner child has developed as a result of your childhood experiences. For instance, you may believe that you are not good enough, worthy of love, safe, or in control. These beliefs and fears may prevent you from living authentically and fulfilling your potential. Challenge those beliefs and fears by telling yourself that you are good enough, worthy, safe, and can always control your own thoughts and emotions. Show your inner child that you are your own hero, and that you will always be there to rescue yourself.

5. **<u>Change your inner child's beliefs and fears</u>**: Replace any negative or limiting beliefs or fears with positive and empowering ones. You can do this by using affirmations, visualizations, journaling, or other techniques that can help you reprogram your subconscious mind. For example, you can say to yourself: "I am good enough," "I am worthy of love," "I am safe," or "I am in control." It also helps to reassure your inner child that the responses you had when you were that little you were perfectly appropriate. It is completely understandable to have felt that way, especially considering the circumstances. Such emotions are valid and natural for a child to experience as well.
6. **<u>Nurture your inner child:</u>** Give your inner child what they need to feel happy, healthy, and fulfilled. You can do this by engaging in activities that bring you joy, creativity, and curiosity and make you playful. You can also express your needs and desires to others and set healthy boundaries. Let your inner child play the way you used to play when you were carefree and exploring your world for the first time.

By nurturing a new inner core for your inner child, you embark on a transformative journey of healing and self-discovery. This process allows you to heal from past wounds, embrace your authentic self, and cultivate a strong sense of self-worth. Through this journey, you can enhance your self-esteem, develop greater self-compassion, boost your self-confidence, and unlock your unique self-expression. Moreover, as you deepen your relationship with yourself, meaningful connections with others will flourish, leading to more fulfilling and authentic relationships. Ultimately, this inner work empowers you to live a life aligned with your true purpose and unleash your full potential.

With the basic concepts in mind, we will now explore some guided exercises to help you build that new core.

Exercise #4

You and Your Inner Child

This exercise will be focused on helping you to reach out to your inner child to better understand the damage they suffered and how you can help them going forward. One of the ways to heal your inner child is to practice a meditative exercise that allows you to connect with your younger self. After you are able to do that successfully, you can progress to healing the pain your inner child suffered with past trauma.

Part 1

Finding Your Inner Child

This exercise will help you to reach out and connect to your inner child. Here are the steps to follow:

1. Find a comfortable and quiet place where you can sit or lie down. Close your eyes and take a few deep breaths to relax your body and mind. Make sure your breaths expand both your belly and your chest.
2. Imagine that you are in a safe and beautiful place, such as a garden, beach, or forest. Feel the warmth of the sun, the breeze of the wind, or the sound of the water. This is your inner sanctuary, where you can meet your inner child.
3. As you explore your inner sanctuary, look for a sign that indicates where your inner child is. It could be a toy, drawing, or symbol. Follow the sign until you find your inner child.
4. Greet your inner child with love and compassion. Notice how they look, what they are wearing, and how they feel. Ask them if they want to talk to or play with you. Respect their wishes and boundaries.

5. Spend some time with your inner child, listening to their stories, feelings, and needs. Validate their emotions and experiences. Tell them that you understand exactly why they feel the way they do and that you are here for them, love them, and are proud of them.
6. When ready, give your inner child a hug and thank them for spending time with you. Tell them that you will come back whenever they need you, will always be on their side, and will always take care of them. Say goodbye and leave them in their safe place.
7. Return to your present awareness by taking a few deep breaths and opening your eyes. Notice how you feel after doing this exercise. Write down any insights or messages that you received from your inner child.

Part 2

Healing Your Inner Child

This exercise can assist you in letting go of any negative emotions, beliefs, or memories that are hindering your ability to reach your full potential. One way to heal the trauma your inner child suffered is to practice a meditative exercise that will connect you with your younger self and offer them compassion and support. This will involve reliving past trauma, so approach this exercise with self-compassion and allow yourself to sit with any of the emotions that arise.

Below is a straightforward step-by-step guide to performing this exercise:

1. **Once more, locate a serene and cozy environment where you can comfortably sit or lie down and unwind:** Close your eyes and take deep breaths, expanding your belly and chest to calm your mind and body.

2. **Imagine you are in that same safe and beautiful place where you first connected with your inner child:** Feel the warmth of the sun, the breeze of the wind, or the sound of the water. This is where you will be meeting them once again.
3. **Call your attention to a past trauma you experienced as a child and visualize your inner child as they were at that time and whatever age they were.** Notice their appearance, expression, emotions, and needs. How do they feel? What do they want to tell you?
4. **Approach your inner child with kindness and gentleness:** Tell them you are here to listen to, comfort, and help them heal. Ask if they would like a hug or touch from you. Respect their boundaries and preferences.
5. **Take the time to listen to your inner child, validating their feelings and experiences:** Give acknowledgment to their pain and suffering and offer apologies for any neglect or abandonment they may have experienced in the past. Express your unconditional love for them and let them know how proud you are of their resilience in surviving the trauma.
6. **Ask your inner child what they need from you now:** Do they need reassurance, protection, guidance, or encouragement? Do they need you to take any action on their behalf? Do they need you to forgive yourself or someone else? Do whatever you can to meet their needs and honor their wishes. The more you can honor their wishes, the better you will be at healing that old trauma.
7. **Thank your inner child for trusting and sharing with you:** Tell them you will always be there for them and that they can come back to this place anytime they want. Reassure them that now that the two of you are fully connected, you will listen to them and respect their needs. Give them another hug or touch if they want it, then gently let them go and return to the present moment.

8. **<u>Open your eyes and take a moment to notice how you feel after doing this exercise:</u>** You may feel more peaceful, compassionate, empowered, or healed. You may also feel some emotions or sensations that need further attention or processing. These can sometimes be extremely painful, but if you allow yourself to sit with the pain and process it, you will notice it changing and dissipating. Don't be afraid to let yourself fully feel whatever arises for you. Whatever you are feeling, accept it without judgment and take care of yourself.

Final Thoughts on Your Inner Child

With a strong connection to your inner child, you will develop a heightened awareness of their needs—don't ignore those. Responding to the needs of your inner child will help them heal. By prioritizing your own needs and demonstrating self-care, you will experience accelerated progress in your healing journey, surpassing what would be possible otherwise. This is what most codependent people have found lacking in their lives. They wanted someone to care about them, but what they really needed was to care about themselves. When you prove to yourself that you will always show up for what you need, you will find that you are ready to embrace all parts of yourself—even those you might find disagreeable.

Chapter 5

Embrace Your Shadow Self

Have you ever met someone that you just disliked instantly? Maybe you didn't like the way they dressed, or perhaps their conduct rubbed you the wrong way. Do you remember the intensity of your dislike? Often, this can be a very strong feeling. I know I've met a few people like that in my life. I even speculated that maybe they had murdered me in a previous life. As I embarked on my personal growth journey, I gained a deeper understanding that the intensity of our dislike toward others often stems from the fear of resemblances between them and ourselves. They are exhibiting some traits that we reject in ourselves. When we see someone acting particularly "bad" or "evil" based on our criteria, we react intensely toward that person; however, we are really just judging what we fear is our own shadow self. To heal and become whole, we must understand and embrace our shadow self. Not only is it an important part of our psyche, but our shadow self also brings us gifts to help us thrive. But what exactly do we mean by the "shadow self?"

What is a Shadow Self?

The shadow self is a term coined by [Swiss psychologist Carl Jung](#) to describe the hidden aspects of our personality that we tend to repress or deny. It can contain both positive and negative traits, including creativity, anger, sexuality, fear, envy, etc., and is not inherently bad or evil; rather, it is a source of potential that we can integrate into our conscious awareness. According to Jung, the shadow self is formed in childhood as a result of social conditioning and personal experiences. Through social conditioning, we identify the aspects of ourselves deemed acceptable and valued by others, while simultaneously rejecting those that are not. That makes sense from the perspective of a social species that must learn how to behave in a group setting. But by repressing what is considered bad or unacceptable, we often create problems for ourselves that manifest in our subconscious attitudes and actions.

The rejected aspects of ourselves are pushed into the unconscious, where they hide in the shadows and thus, form the shadow self. The shadow self can influence our thoughts, feelings, and behaviors in ways that we are unaware of, often causing problems and conflicts in our lives. Jung believed that the shadow self can be accessed through dreams, fantasies, art, and other forms of expression. He also advocated for a process of individuation, which involves confronting and accepting our shadow self as part of our wholeness. By doing so, we can gain a deeper understanding of ourselves and others and unleash our creative potential. The shadow self is not something to be feared or avoided; rather, it is a challenge and opportunity for personal growth. Let's look a little more closely at just how this side of yourself forms.

How Does Your Shadow Form?

The shadow self contains all the traits, emotions, thoughts, and impulses that we consider unacceptable, immoral, shameful, or negative. For example, if we believe that being angry is bad, we might suppress our anger and eventually project it onto others. If we think being selfish is wrong, we might hide our needs and desires while resenting those who express theirs. The shadow self forms as a result of our socialization and upbringing. From an early age, we learn what is acceptable and what is not in our family, culture, religion, and society. We internalize these norms and try to conform to them in order to gain approval, love, and belonging. However, this also means we have to repress or disown parts of ourselves that do not fit into these expectations. These parts become our shadow self, which remains hidden in our unconscious mind.

The shadow self can manifest in various ways:

❖ Projection

We attribute our negative qualities or feelings to others without realizing they are actually reflections of ourselves. We might accuse someone of being dishonest when *we* are already lying to ourselves.

❖ Compensation

We overemphasize or exaggerate certain positive qualities or behaviors to cover up or balance out our shadow self. We might act overly generous or altruistic when we are secretly feeling greedy or selfish.

❖ Reaction formation

We express the opposite of what we really feel or think, usually in an exaggerated or extreme way. For example, we might act overly friendly or polite when we actually dislike or resent someone.

❖ Repression

We push down or ignore our shadow self, pretending that it does not exist or that it does not affect us. We might deny having any negative feelings or thoughts, even when they are obvious to others.

The shadow self can cause us various problems as well:

1. **Inner conflict:** We feel torn between our conscious self and our shadow self, which brings us anxiety, guilt, shame, confusion, or dissatisfaction.
2. **Self-sabotage:** Our hidden fears, doubts, or insecurities often manifest unconsciously, leading us to undermine our goals, relationships, or well-being through our actions.
3. **Projection:** We blame others for our own faults or mistakes, creating resentment, hostility, or misunderstanding.
4. **Disconnection:** We lose touch with our authentic self and true potential because we are afraid to face or embrace our shadow self.

Why Should We Integrate the Shadow Self?

The shadow self can also be a source of growth, creativity, and transformation. By becoming aware of and integrating our shadow self, we can achieve wholeness. We can accept and embrace all parts of ourselves, both light and dark, fostering harmony, balance, and peace within ourselves. We also increase self-awareness, helping us gain a deeper understanding of ourselves and recognize our strengths and weaknesses. This self-awareness empowers us to make improvements and learn valuable lessons from our mistakes.

This kind of work allows us to enhance relationships. Through this process, we develop an appreciation for both the differences and similarities among individuals, nurturing trust, respect, and intimacy. Furthermore, as we acknowledge our own needs and prioritize self-care, our relationships with others can be positively influenced. This work also has the potential to unlock creativity by tapping into our hidden talents and passions, enabling us to freely and authentically express ourselves. The result is a life enriched by self-expression and the ability to inspire others.

To integrate our shadow self, we need to:

1. **Acknowledge its existence:** We admit that we have a shadow self and that it influences us in various ways.
2. **Explore its contents:** We examine the traits, emotions, thoughts, and impulses that make up our shadow self and where they come from.
3. **Understand its purpose:** We realize our shadow self is not evil or bad; rather, it is a natural and necessary part of ourselves.
4. **Accept its value:** We appreciate that our shadow self has something to teach and offer us if we listen to and learn from it.
5. **Express its energy:** We find healthy and constructive ways to channel our shadow self into creative outlets or positive actions.

Some examples of what it looks like when you integrate your shadow self include the following:

- A person who represses their anger can learn to assert themselves more effectively and stand up for their rights without being aggressive or violent. They can learn that it's okay to be angry, and they can learn healthy, constructive ways to express that anger.
- A person who compensates for their insecurity by being arrogant or boastful can learn to be more humble and confident without being self-centered. Through this process, individuals are empowered to assess their strengths and weaknesses with a greater sense of honesty, recognizing that their weaknesses do not define their entire identity. Moreover, they can proactively seek ways to enhance areas in which they desire improvement.
- In their pursuit of self-love, individuals who experience codependency may often suppress their own needs. However, they have the opportunity to cultivate self-love by redirecting their focus inward and prioritizing their own

needs as a genuine expression of that love. Doing so will help them develop stronger, healthier, more compassionate, and more loving relationships with other people in their life. By integrating the shadow self, we can achieve a more balanced and authentic sense of who we are and what we want in life. The benefits of this integration include the following.

❖ It Improves All of Our Relationships

Integrating the shadow self can improve our relationships with others and ourselves. By acknowledging and owning up to our shadow traits, we reduce the tendency to blame, judge, or criticize others for what we dislike in ourselves. We can also develop more empathy and compassion for others who struggle with similar issues. Moreover, we increase our self-esteem by embracing all parts of ourselves—not just the ones we deem acceptable or desirable.

❖ It Enhances Our Personal Growth and Development

Another benefit of integration is that it can enhance our personal growth and development. By exploring and understanding our shadow traits, we can discover new aspects of ourselves that we may have neglected or suppressed. We can also learn from our mistakes and challenges and use them as opportunities for growth and transformation. Furthermore, we can unleash our creative potential and express ourselves more fully and authentically.

❖ It Improves Our Overall Well-Being and Happiness

Integrating the shadow elements of our psyche increases our psychological well-being and happiness. By embracing our shadow self, we alleviate the inner conflict and tension that emerges from denying or disregarding aspects of ourselves. We can also liberate ourselves from the fear of being exposed or rejected by others due to us just being ourselves. Additionally, we can align our actions and values with our true selves, empowering us to pursue our goals and dreams with heightened confidence and passion.

You have to know that integrating the shadow self is not an easy or quick process: it requires courage, honesty, and a willingness to face our dark side and embrace it with love and compassion. However, it is a worthwhile and rewarding journey that can help us become more whole, mature, and fulfilled human beings. It can be difficult, but it is, in the end, a fulfilling one.

❖ How Can We Integrate Our Shadow Self?

The shadow self is not inherently bad or evil; it is simply a part of our wholeness that we have not integrated into our conscious awareness, and it can also contain positive qualities that we have neglected or undervalued, such as creativity, spontaneity or intuition. Integrating the shadow self is becoming more aware of and accepting the parts of ourselves that we previously rejected or ignored. This can help us achieve greater balance, authenticity, and harmony within ourselves and with others. Incorporating the shadow self can also unleash our hidden potential, allowing us to express ourselves more fully and freely.

There are many ways to integrate the shadow self, but here are some basic concepts that can be helpful for integration:

1. **Identify your shadow self:** The first step is to recognize the signs of your shadow self in your thoughts, feelings, behaviors, and relationships. To achieve this, it would involve acknowledging the triggers, projections, judgments,

insecurities, or recurring patterns contributing to your distress or discomfort. Additionally, utilizing techniques like journaling, meditation, dream analysis, or psychological tests can aid in delving into your unconscious mind and revealing hidden aspects of your shadow self. Strong emotional triggers can serve as a valuable signal indicating the presence of your shadow self, which you may unconsciously project into your unconscious mind. Think of it like this: when you push down on dough when making bread, it doesn't disappear; rather, it squishes around your hands and fingers. The shadow does the same thing. You can't banish it from existence—it simply hides in the darkness, affecting your behavior in the background. Identifying it means finding it in the hidden recesses of your psyche and bringing it into the light.

2. **Acknowledge and accept your shadow self:** The second step is to face your shadow self with honesty and compassion. Instead of denying, avoiding, or resisting your shadow aspects, try to understand and accept them as part of who you are. You can do this by expressing your feelings safely and healthily through writing, talking, or art. You can also practice self-compassion and forgiveness with yourself and others who may have contributed to your shadow formation. Basically, your shadow self wants to step into the light and be seen. By embracing your shadow self with love and acceptance, you unlock the myriad of gifts it holds, even though it may have been hidden until now.

3. **Transform your shadow self:** The third step is to transform your shadow self into a source of strength and growth. Instead of letting your shadow control or limit you, try to learn from and use them for your benefit. You can do this by finding positive ways to channel your shadow energy, such as through creativity, passion, or courage. You can also seek to balance your shadow aspects with their opposite qualities,

such as kindness, generosity, or humility. Every shadow brings with it a gift; your selfish shadow self just wants you to have what you want and need in life. Your greedy shadow self is trying to secure your needs for the rest of your life, and your angry shadow self is expressing a need for a boundary. Within every shadow resides a hidden gift, as each shadow represents a part of yourself that is seeking to assist you in its own unique way. It can help you not just survive, but thrive. By acknowledging this truth, you can embark on a transformative journey where the once-feared shadow evolves from a menacing figure in your nightmares to a heroic presence in your most cherished dreams.

Integrating the shadow self is not a one-time event but a lifelong journey of self-discovery and personal development. There may be many times in your life when you will have to revisit the shadows that have formed in your psyche. It can be challenging and uncomfortable at times—maybe even painful—but it can also be rewarding and liberating. By integrating the shadow self, you become more aware of yourself and others, authentic and confident, compassionate and empathetic, creative and expressive, adaptable and resilient, and whole and complete. Your shadow self is an important part of you, and once you acknowledge and accept its existence, then can you use the gifts it brings to your advantage.

Exercise #5

In the Shadows of Your Mind

One of the most important steps in personal growth is identifying and integrating your shadow self. The first part of this exercise focuses on identifying those shadow elements of yourself. The second part will focus on integrating your shadow selves into the entirety of your identity.

Part 1

You and Your Shadow

To identify your shadow self, you need to be willing to face the parts of yourself that you may not like or accept. A simple exercise to do this is to write down a list of traits you admire or despise in others. For example, you may admire someone's courage, creativity, or generosity, or you may despise someone's arrogance, dishonesty, or selfishness.

Then, for each trait, ask yourself the following questions:

- How does this trait show up in me?
- Do I believe this trait is positive or negative?
- Where did I learn to judge this trait in that way?
- What other characteristics do I associate with this trait?
- How do I express or suppress this trait?
- How does this trait serve or hinder me?

Be honest and compassionate with yourself as you explore these questions. By engaging in this exercise, you acknowledge and embrace your shadow self, leading to a deeper understanding of it and greater self-acceptance. You can harness the power and wisdom of your shadow self instead of fearing or shaming it.

Part 2

Bring Your Shadow into the Light

Integrating the shadow self is becoming more aware, accepting, and compassionate of these aspects of ourselves. Here is a meditative exercise that can help you with this process:

1. Return to that serene and tranquil space where you can comfortably sit or recline. Close your eyes and take 10 deep

breaths that expand both your chest and your belly. Relax your body and mind.
2. Bring to your awareness a situation or person that triggers a strong negative emotion in you, such as anger, jealousy, shame, or guilt. Pay attention to the sensations and emotions that arise within your body and mind when you contemplate this situation or person. Take note of where you feel the emotional response and the quality of the sensation that arises.
3. Can you identify a reason for your strong emotional response? Maybe you don't like that they are arrogant because your mother always told you that old Biblical adage, "Pride goeth before a fall." Determine just what creates the strong reaction you feel.
4. Ask yourself: What part of me is being activated by this situation or person? Is this an old wound? Is it part of an internalized belief system? What does this part of me want or need? How does it relate to my shadow self?
5. Visualize a distinct manifestation of this aspect of yourself as if it were standing right in front of you. Observe its appearance, posture, expression, and energy. Can you see that shadow hiding away in a corner of your mind? Try not to judge or criticize it but simply acknowledge its presence.
6. Start a dialogue with this part of you. Ask it questions like: What is your name? What is your purpose? What are you trying to tell me? What do you need from me? Approach this inner entity with a sense of curiosity and openness, listening attentively to its responses. Allow the answers to emerge within you without passing any judgment. Maintain an open mind and a sincere intention to establish a connection with this aspect of yourself.
7. Think honestly about the intentions behind your shadow self. It is possible that this part of yourself represents suppressed anger or rage. Why is this shadow angry? How does that

rage serve you? For example, I struggled with my own shadow self related to anger. My mother had always made it clear that I should never show anger, so I repressed this side of myself. But what does anger give us? Anger serves as a protective tool, helping us set boundaries, meet our needs, and address unfair situations. It can motivate us to take action and promote personal growth when expressed appropriately. Examine the intentions behind your shadow's actions and understand them from the perspective of that part of yourself, acknowledging that it was attempting to serve your best interests.

8. Express your gratitude and appreciation toward this aspect of yourself—its presence and the lessons it has provided. Show appreciation for its role in your growth and healing process. Tell it that you accept it and love it unconditionally and reassure that you understand the intentions behind its influence on your thoughts and behavior. Let it know that you realize it has always been on your side and that you want it to come into the light.

9. Imagine yourself embracing and merging it with your whole being. Feel that wholeness and completeness that arises from integrating your shadow self, and observing any changes in your energy, emotions, or overall well-being. Allow yourself to fully embody this sense of inner alignment and cherish the newfound harmony within you. I was able to incorporate expressing anger healthily so I could set firm boundaries and prevent further abuse.

10. Once you have embraced your shadow self, bring your attention back to your breaths; take 10 more deep breaths that expand both your belly and chest. As you do so, express love and gratitude for your courage in facing the darkness inside of you and bringing it into the light. Open your eyes and reflect on your experience. Write down any insights or messages you received from your shadow self.

Final Thoughts Up to This Point

With a deeper awareness of the origins of your learned patterns of behaviors, thoughts, and emotions, along with your efforts to heal your inner child and integrate your shadows, you may now be experiencing a range of transformative changes. Do not fear these changes; they are natural and anticipated. Throughout this half of the book, you have engaged in substantial personal growth work. It is likely that you have encountered a multitude of emotions, and it is understandable to feel somewhat disoriented amidst it all. Remember that healing is a gradual process, and it takes time for old wounds to mend completely. This first half of the book has been focused on identifying your patterns of thinking and behavior associated with your codependency. These could have been wounds that created your core beliefs, emotional triggers that formed from your childhood wounds, pain of your inner child, and parts of yourself you relegated to the shadows.

Let yourself experience the changes you're going through and sit with the emotions that come up while continuing to use these techniques to heal. Now it's time to also look at how this process can help you grow into a healthier, happier person. We want to explore how to recognize and prioritize your own needs and why doing so will help make your relationships better. As codependents, we often derive our values from the support we give to other people, but that's a hollow kind of value. True self-value has to come from within—not without. The progress you have made thus far empowers you to embrace these changes and integrate them into your life, fostering personal growth and improvement. You can truly become your own hero—your own Prince or Princess Charming—who will arrive to save the day. When you do, you will discover the beauty of your unique essence, which will be how you create the life you've always dreamed of having.

Chapter 6

Becoming Your Own Hero

What is a hero? This can mean different things to different people. I have a friend who was a teenager in the mid-70s when the movie *Alien*, starring Sigourney Weaver, came out. She was very impressed by this movie because it challenged the stereotype of women in horror movies. Weaver was strong, assertive, and saved herself when no one else could or would. She was not a people-pleaser; she did what needed to be done, and when no one else would listen, she saved herself. In the sequel to that movie, *Aliens*, Weaver revives her role as Ripley and once again plays a stereotype-breaking character as she saves a little girl with the nickname Newt. In one scene, Ripley is holding Newt in her arms as she comes face-to-face with the queen alien creature. It is huge and seems indestructible, but Ripley, though terrified, does not let that stop her, and she ultimately saves them both.

As my friend grew older and began her own healing journey, that's how she envisioned herself in her mind's eye—she was that strong, determined, assertive, and gloriously beautiful woman holding her inner child in her arms as she stood before the seemingly indestructible monsters from her childhood. And she ultimately—same as Ripley—saved them both. You might not be facing a flesh-and-blood, acid-dripping alien from outer space, but your monsters are equally as frightening and may be seemingly as indestructible. Still, you can stand strong with your inner child in your arms and your army of shadow selves as you vanquish them from your lived experience. That's what I call a hero.

Becoming Ripley

Having embarked on the journey of healing your codependency, the next step involves engaging in healthy interactions with others. This entails acquiring the necessary skills to establish boundaries that align with your newfound self-respect and self-love. Embrace the opportunity to fulfill the promise you made to your inner child, becoming the hero they longed for. Let's explore the transformative process of shifting from codependency to independence—from being a people-pleaser to embodying the spirit of Ripley. To begin, we have to recognize what healthy relationships look like; after all, you've been codependent for so long, so it can be difficult to know how to identify emotionally mature ways of interacting with the people you love.

What Exactly is a Healthy Relationship?

A healthy relationship is based on mutual respect, trust, support, and communication. It allows both partners to have their own interests, hobbies, and friends, and both parties should be able to grow as individuals. A healthy relationship does not involve excessive control, manipulation, guilt, or sacrifice. It does not make you feel anxious, frustrated, or pitying of your partner, nor does it mean neglecting your own needs in favor of pleasing others. Interacting with other people is an essential part of human life; however, not all interactions are healthy or beneficial for our well-being. So what exactly characterizes a healthy interaction?

1. **Communication is Key:** It all begins with communication. Healthy interactions with other people require you to communicate clearly and respectfully. This means expressing your thoughts, feelings and needs honestly,

politely, and for what is appropriate for the situation. Communication also involves listening actively and empathetically to what others have to say and acknowledging their perspectives and emotions. Active listening means to consider thoughtfully what the other person says. Doing so allows you to see their perspective more clearly. By communicating respectfully, you avoid misunderstandings, conflicts, and hurt feelings while building trust and rapport with others.

2. **<u>Setting Boundaries is Required:</u>** Another healthy way of interacting with other people is to set boundaries and respect them. Boundaries define the scope of our personal space and the standards we establish for ourselves and others regarding our comfort levels and mutual expectations. They can be physical, emotional, or social and can vary depending on the context and relationship. Setting boundaries helps us protect our personal space, privacy, and autonomy while preventing us from being exploited or manipulated by others. Respecting boundaries means honoring the choices and preferences of others and not imposing your values or expectations on them. Setting boundaries, however, also shows respect for yourself. You are listening to your inner child and respecting your own needs. When you set a boundary with someone else, that's a way of saying that you respect yourself and expect them to do the same.

3. **<u>Giving and Receiving Feedback is Necessary:</u>** A third healthy way of interacting with other people is giving and receiving constructive feedback. Feedback refers to the valuable insights we receive from others regarding our performance or behavior, highlighting areas where we excel or have room for improvement. It can encompass both positive and constructive aspects, and its effectiveness lies in being specific, relevant, and delivered in a timely manner.

Giving constructive feedback means providing honest and helpful suggestions for improvement without being harsh or judgmental. Receiving constructive feedback means accepting it as an opportunity to learn and grow without becoming defensive or resentful. It can be tricky to accomplish this without offending other people or yourself. The Buddhists say that before saying anything to someone else, you should consider three questions: Is it necessary, is it kind, and is it true? If you can't answer yes to all three, then it's better not to say it. Even if you have to say something that might be negative, you should strive to say it kindly. Others should do the same for you, and if they don't, then you will want to consider carefully their intentions and your relationship with them. Someone who loves and respects you should not want to hurt you.

What About Interacting in Conflicts?

Conflict is inevitable in any relationship, whether it is with a friend, family member, partner, or colleague. However, conflict does not have to be destructive or damaging. In fact, conflict can be an opportunity to learn, grow, and strengthen the bond between two people. The key is to interact healthily during a conflict, which means respecting each other's feelings, needs, and perspectives while avoiding behaviors that can escalate the situation or cause harm.

To avoid that, before engaging in a conflict, take a moment to calm yourself and assess the situation. Ask yourself what the issue is, what you want to achieve from the conversation, and what emotions you are feeling. Doing so can help you avoid reacting impulsively or defensively and prepare you for more constructive dialogue. Use "I" statements instead of "you" statements when expressing your feelings and needs to avoid a "blaming" tone. For example, instead of saying, "You always ignore me when I talk to you," you can say, "I feel hurt when you don't pay attention to me." The other person will become more receptive to your message if you don't make it sound like you're blaming them. Listen actively and empathetically to the other person's point of view and try to understand where they are coming from, what they are feeling, and what they need. Don't interrupt, judge them, or dismiss them; show that you are paying attention by nodding, making eye contact, and paraphrasing what they said.

Another important thing to do is to focus on the problem, not the person. Avoid personal attacks, insults, name-calling, or generalizations. Don't bring up past issues or unrelated topics; stick to the facts and the current situation. Instead of saying, "You're such a lazy and selfish person," you can say, "I'm frustrated that you didn't do your share of the project." Seek to understand before being understood, and don't assume that you know what the other person is thinking or feeling. You never know what may have caused their behavior. Ask open-ended questions to clarify their position and show interest in their perspective. For example, "Can you tell me more about why you did that?" or "How did that make you feel?" might work well. Look for common ground and solutions that benefit both parties rather than viewing the conversation as an opportunity to prove that you are right. Some examples of statements you can try include, "I agree that we both want to do a good job on this project" and "How can we make this work for both of us?"

It's also vital to respect the other person's boundaries and preferences. Give them the freedom to choose when they are ready and comfortable to engage in conversation and avoid placing undue pressure on them to conform to your viewpoint or alter their beliefs. Respect their personal boundaries and refrain from intruding upon their privacy or personal space.

Also respect their right to have different opinions and feelings than yours; it's important to expect them to do the same for you. If they are not doing that, you might need to end the conversation until things have calmed down and everyone can behave respectfully. Of course, you also need to apologize if you hurt or offend the other person. Acknowledge your mistakes and take responsibility for your actions. Express regret and sincerity for what you did or said—you can try these: "I'm sorry for raising my voice at you" or "I apologize for being insensitive to your feelings." When you are respectful to them, it makes it easier to end the conversation on a positive note. Thank the other person for listening and sharing their thoughts with you and express appreciation and gratitude for their efforts and cooperation. Affirm your relationship and commitment to each other with things like "I'm glad we had this talk," "I value our friendship," or "I love you." By expressing appreciation and gratitude, you cultivate a healthy and positive dynamic in your interactions, which has the potential to strengthen both your personal and professional relationships. Moreover, practicing gratitude can contribute to an elevated sense of self-worth and overall happiness. Doing this regularly can help you develop more effective communication, collaboration, and conflict resolution abilities and foster a positive social environment for yourself and others.

Self-Care is Vital for Going from Codependent to Independent

Self-care can help you reduce stress, boost your self-esteem, and increase your independence. It's the one thing that most codependents neglect for themselves; they put other people ahead of their own needs, sometimes to the extent of it being detrimental to their health and well-being.

Self-care practices are essential for maintaining one's physical, mental, and emotional health. They can help reduce stress, improve mood, enhance productivity, and foster resilience. However, many people struggle to find time or motivation to practice self-care regularly. In particular, self-care can boost your immune system and prevent illness. When you take care of your body by eating well, exercising, sleeping enough, and avoiding harmful substances, you are strengthening your natural defenses against infections and diseases. Moreover, practicing self-care can aid in managing chronic conditions such as diabetes, hypertension, or arthritis, allowing you to effectively address symptoms and enhance your overall quality of life.

Another benefit of self-care is that it can improve your mental health and emotional stability. When you take care of your mind by engaging in activities that make you happy, relaxed, and fulfilled, you are reducing stress, anxiety, and depression levels. You are also increasing your self-esteem, confidence, and optimism by acknowledging your strengths and achievements. Furthermore, self-care can help you build healthy relationships with others by enhancing your communication skills, empathy, and compassion.

Here are some of the tips for practicing self-care:

- Set realistic and attainable goals for yourself and celebrate your progress.
- Schedule some time for yourself every day to do something you enjoy or learn something new.
- Seek professional help when you need it and reach out to your support network when you feel lonely or overwhelmed.
- Practice gratitude for what you have and appreciation for those who matter to you.
- Be mindful of your thoughts and feelings and accept them without judgment.
- Practice relaxation techniques such as breathing exercises, meditation, or yoga.
- Say no to things that drain your energy or violate your boundaries.

- Ask for help when you need it and delegate tasks when possible.

It's important to remember that self-care practices are not selfish or indulgent—they are necessary and beneficial for your overall well-being. By taking care of yourself, you are also taking care of others who depend on or care about you. Therefore, make self-care a priority in your life and enjoy the positive outcomes that come with it.

A Word About Seeking Professional Help

If you are struggling with codependency, you may benefit from seeking help from a mental health professional who can provide you with support, guidance, and tools to overcome your challenges. I began my own healing journey this way, and I'm so glad I did. My therapist really helped me see the truth of my codependency and learn how to heal from it. A therapist can help you identify the root causes of your codependency, challenge your negative beliefs and patterns, and teach you new skills and strategies to cope with your emotions and the situation you're in. A therapist can also assist you in establishing objectives for yourself and your relationship, as well as monitoring your advancement and accomplishments.

Seeking out therapy when you need it is not a sign of weakness—it's actually the opposite. It requires courage, commitment, and patience. It also requires a willingness to change yourself and your relationships for the better. To face the demons of your own psyche—the monsters born of childhood trauma—you genuinely have to be a hero. To ask a therapist for help is part of the heroic actions that even Ripley took to deal with the trauma her monsters inflicted. You should not feel even a tinge of shame when you ask for professional help. You should feel proud of yourself for being brave enough to seek out this beneficial form of healthcare.

Another compelling reason to seek professional assistance is that this behavioral pattern often leads to the development of addictions stemming from the prevalent anxiety experienced by codependent individuals. Codependency itself is a type of addiction—an addiction to relationships. Most codependents feel extreme anxiety associated with their fear of losing those they love and the problems that stem from their own low self-esteem. To quell that anxiety, it's not uncommon to turn to substances, food, or behaviors like gambling or excessive use of social media, which would take them away from their inner turmoil. To conquer these addictions, it is crucial to engage the guidance of a professional who can aid you in discovering healthier coping mechanisms and fostering the necessary self-esteem to steer clear of addictive behaviors.

One thing to realize about healing is that it takes time, usually years. It's a long journey, but absolutely worth every second. I remember that many nights as I was going through therapy, I could not sleep. I found myself talking to my mother inside my head as a kid—not as my adult self. I was trying to explain my feelings and blame her for the trauma she inflicted on me. On many occasions, as my wounds healed, I would feel intense pain. I felt anxious and often had destructive thoughts. I even tried to talk to my mom over the phone about what I was going through and my insights. The response? "You've gone crazy with your psychology!"

That's pretty typical. She couldn't understand any of it, and like many perpetrators—who are themselves wounded—she didn't want to understand it. I had to learn to accept her as she was: complete with her current mindset and values. It's hard to feel close to someone with whom you don't share the same values anymore. Grateful for her role as my mother and the gift of life, I appreciate even her devaluation and criticism, recognizing that they have shaped me into the person I am today. With time, I not only forgave her, but I also forgave myself for prioritizing my mother over myself. I created my own inner, supportive, loving mom—the mother I never really had. In doing so, I restored my shine and inner power. It took six years of occasionally excruciating and difficult personal growth work, but I now feel complete within myself. You can achieve this too. Just don't give up; seek out whatever type of care it is you need to reach your potential.

Stop Comparing Yourself to Others

One of the most common sources of unhappiness and stress in our lives, particularly those of us who are codependent, is the habit of comparing ourselves to other people. Whether it's about our appearance, achievements, relationships, or possessions, we often feel inadequate or dissatisfied when we see someone else who seems to have it better than us. But this habit is not only harmful to our mental and emotional well-being—it also prevents us from appreciating and developing our own unique strengths and talents. Comparing ourselves to others can lead to a distorted sense of reality and loss of self-esteem. We may forget that everyone has their own struggles and challenges and that what we see on the surface is not the whole truth. We may also overlook how we are all different and have different goals, values, and preferences. What works for one person may not work for us, and vice versa. By constantly measuring ourselves against others, we are setting ourselves up for disappointment and frustration.

The pervasive comparison culture, fueled by the surge of social media, has reached epidemic proportions. While social media has become deeply ingrained in our lives, its dark side manifests in the form of feelings of inadequacy and unhappiness. Constant exposure to unrealistic standards and idealized portrayals of others' lives on social media contributes to these negative emotions. This phenomenon is known as social comparison, and it can have negative effects on our mental health and well-being. One definition of social comparison is the tendency to evaluate ourselves in relation to others, either by looking up to those who seem better than us (upward comparison) or looking down on those who seem worse than us (downward comparison). Although some degree of social comparison is natural and inevitable, social media has amplified it to unhealthy levels. Social media platforms are built to incentivize users to showcase their accomplishments, viewpoints, and moments, but in the process, they construct a distorted and curated version of reality. We only see the highlights of other people's lives—not the struggles, failures, and challenges they face. We also tend to compare ourselves to people who are similar to us in some way, such as age, gender, or profession, which makes the comparison more salient and impactful.

Engaging in social comparison through social media can have negative consequences on our self-esteem, mood, and motivation. Research has shown that frequent exposure to social media can increase feelings of envy, dissatisfaction, loneliness, and depression. It can also lower our self-confidence, self-acceptance, and self-worth. Moreover, it can reduce our ability to appreciate what we have and enjoy our achievements. Instead of focusing on our own goals and values, we may chase external validation and approval from others. How can we cope effectively with the epidemic of social comparison? One approach is to consciously limit our time and engagement with social media, practicing mindfulness, and being selective in what we consume and share online. But there is more we can do.

Instead of comparing ourselves to others, we should be focusing on our own growth and improvement. We should celebrate our achievements—no matter how big or small—and learn from our mistakes. We should recognize our strengths and work on our weaknesses. We should appreciate and value what we have and what we can do instead of dwelling on what we lack or cannot achieve. By doing so, we boost our confidence and happiness and become more resilient and adaptable to life's challenges. Comparing ourselves to others is a natural human tendency, but healthy nor productive. It can steal our happiness and potential, leaving us feeling inferior or envious. Instead of wasting our time and energy on comparing ourselves to others, we should invest them in becoming the best version of ourselves. This way, we will not only improve our own lives but also inspire and help others along the way.

Codependency and Comparison

Codependents often fixate on people who seem to have more happiness, success, or love than they do, and may be doing so to compare themselves to others and seek validation, approval, or acceptance from them. They may also use comparison as a way of avoiding their problems or feelings of inadequacy. However, this strategy often backfires, as it only reinforces their negative self-image and makes them feel more insecure and unhappy.

You can overcome the habit of comparing yourself to others with the following tips:

1. **Challenge distorted beliefs:** This is recognizing and challenging distorted thoughts and beliefs making you feel inferior or unworthy.
1. **Practice gratitude:** Foster appreciation for what you have and recognize your strengths and achievements.
2. **Focus on Your Goals:** Prioritize your goals and values, directing your attention toward them rather than being preoccupied with the thoughts and actions of others.
3. **Surround Yourself with Supportive Family and Friends:** Especially when you participate often in social media, it can be difficult to find genuinely supportive friends and family members who have your best interests at heart. Surrounding yourself with loving and supportive friends and family is the best way to recognize all your good characteristics and stop comparing yourself to other people.

4. **Join a Support Group:** CoDA or Codependents Anonymous offers a valuable support network for codependents, providing a platform to listen to the experiences of others and share your own journey. This supportive environment can aid in your personal growth, helping you overcome codependency and break free from the cycle of comparison to others.

Embracing self-love and self-respect empowers you to let go of comparisons and embrace your unique journey. By focusing on your own path and embracing authenticity and joy, you can break free from the trap of constantly comparing yourself to others. When you do that, you also learn to prioritize your own needs and goals. The truth is that when you finally advocate for yourself and become your own hero, that's when you can finally start forming the loving and mutually respectful relationships you've wanted all along. It sounds cliche, but the key to loving others really is learning to love yourself.

Exercise #6

Ripley Fights Back

Becoming your own superhero involves two key aspects: establishing healthy boundaries and embracing your individual journey without comparing yourself to others. By setting effective boundaries and living authentically, you can empower yourself to be the hero of your own story. The following exercises are focused on helping you to do that.

Part 1

It's All About Boundaries

For this exercise, you will be using the acronym BOUND: Be clear, Own your feelings, Understand your needs, Negotiate respectfully, and Decide on consequences. Here is a rundown of what each letter in the acronym means:

1. **B stands for Be Clear :** Once again, go to your quiet place where you will not be disturbed. Reflect on each part of your life. You don't have to do this all at once; you can choose a different part of your life to focus on over the course of several days or weeks. Write down what you want and don't want in a specific situation or relationship. For example, "I want to spend time with my friends without feeling guilty" or "I don't want to lend money to my brother anymore." You should be as specific as you can be for each situation and relationship.
2. **is for Own Your Feelings**: Take a moment to recognize your emotions when your boundaries are either violated or honored. Reflect on how you feel in specific situations, such as "I experience frustration when my boss expects me to work additional hours without fair compensation" or "I feel appreciated and content when my partner values and respects my opinions." By acknowledging your emotions, you gain insight into what is lacking and can identify your needs more clearly.
3. **U Stands for Understand Your Needs:** Once you have a clear understanding of your emotions related to your boundaries, take the time to identify the specific needs that contribute to your sense of safety, comfort, and respect. For instance, you might realize that you require privacy and personal space in order to feel at ease, or that honest communication is necessary for maintaining healthy

relationships with your family. Being specific about your needs is essential as it paves the way for the next step in the process.

4. **N is for Negotiate Respectfully:** Effectively communicating your boundaries to others requires a calm and assertive approach. For instance, you can express your needs by saying, "I appreciate your invitation, but I'm unable to join you tonight. I need some personal time" or "I'm sorry, but I can't continue lending you money. It's not beneficial for our relationship." It's important to note that setting boundaries doesn't require you to be angry; it's simply about respecting yourself and encouraging others to do the same. By calmly stating your needs and limits, you prioritize your well-being and ensure a more impactful message is conveyed.

5. **Decide on Consequences:** It is important to have a plan of action if your boundaries are violated or ignored. Consider the following examples: "If you continue to call me after 10 pm, I will block your number," or "If you fail to repay me by next week, I will take legal action." Similarly, you could say, "If you yell at me, I will leave and cease communication until you can speak to me respectfully," or "If you engage in physical harm, I will contact the authorities." In certain situations, it may be beneficial to document your boundaries and consequences in writing to ensure clarity and prevent any claims of unawareness. The specific actions and approach may vary depending on the nature of the relationship.

This exercise can help you practice setting strong boundaries and improve your self-esteem and well-being. It's you respecting yourself. Once you have identified your boundaries and needs, you can then communicate them to the people you believe are common violators. You can also communicate your boundaries to those who already respect them. Express your appreciation for their actions and let them know that their example has motivated you to assert these boundaries with others in your life who may not be respecting them. People who respect you will be happy you're taking this step.

Part 2

Living Your Unique Path

Comparing your experiences to others can lead to feelings of inadequacy, envy, and dissatisfaction with your own achievements and qualities, especially when you come across someone who appears to have a better situation than you. However, this habit is not only unhelpful but also unrealistic. Everyone has their own strengths and weaknesses, challenges and opportunities, and goals and values. No two people are exactly alike, and no one has a perfect life. Thus, comparing ourselves to others is like comparing apples to oranges; it does not make sense, and it does not serve us well.

One exercise to help you stop comparing yourself with others and appreciate your unique path in life is as follows:

1. **Notice the Good:** Sit in your quiet area and reflect honestly on your experiences thus far in life. Make a list of things you're proud of, enjoy doing, are skilled at, and grateful for.
2. **Make a List:** Write down 10 positive affirmations that remind you of your value and potential. Consider the following examples as baselines for your own affirmations:

❖ "I am enough"
❖ "I have something to offer to the world"
❖ "I am worthy of love and respect"
❖ "I can achieve my goals"
❖ "I have my own unique path and it is incredible"

3. **Assess Your Limitations Honestly:** Next, list any limitations that may be preventing you from achieving your goals. Maybe you need to go to school and can't afford it

right now, or perhaps you want to express yourself musically but don't know how to play an instrument.
4. **Make Another List:** Now, make a list of 10 affirmations related to the limitations you noted. Consider the following examples when starting out your list:

- "I am so much more than any limitation."
- "Nothing can stop me from achieving my happiness because I am my happiness."

Then, if you want to go to school but can't afford it, you might write, "I am intelligent and can express that in many ways." If you don't know how to play an instrument, you might write, "The music I *can* express is in my soul." Another good one is, "My limitations don't prevent me from experiencing joy," or "I am like water; I can move around any obstacle in my path." Limitations are only temporary obstacles; they don't really prevent us from moving along our unique path because there is always a way around them.

We can regularly review and update this list, allowing it to serve as a powerful tool to boost our confidence, motivation, and overall happiness. Through this exercise, we come to recognize and appreciate our inherent value and our ability to make positive contributions to the world, regardless of our current circumstances.

Final Thoughts on Saving Yourself

One of the most important things about being your own hero is learning to respect and love yourself. You have value and understanding that will unlock your potential. Once you can set your own boundaries and express them to others—and stop living your life as a comparison to others—then can you resolve those old, toxic relationships and move toward what can really make you happy. These are concepts we will explore in the coming chapters.

Chapter 7

Resolving Old, Toxic Relationships

Toxic relationships are commonly viewed as negative influences or individuals who have entered our lives. However, it is worth considering an alternative perspective: What if these relationships could be opportunities for growth and learning? What if we turn it around and make them lessons that enable us to tap into our unlimited potential? How would knowing that change your perception of those toxic relationships? How would it change your codependency? No one else's experience is any less valid than another's. Would knowing that change the way you interact with other people?

For a significant period, I found myself constantly comparing my experiences to those of others, passing judgment along the way. That's not uncommon; almost everyone does that. Upon realizing the toxicity of my narcissistic husband, I couldn't help but feel empathy toward him, recognizing my own toxic behavioral patterns and sensing the torturous state of his mind and underlying fragility. But that doesn't change the fact that I also knew I had to get away from him—I had to get out of that relationship. And what did that represent for me? It meant that I was finally understanding on some level that I didn't deserve that kind of treatment. That's a big insight to have, even though I clearly didn't see it that way at the time. And who sparked that insight in me? It was none other than my toxic husband.

I also realized that I was judging his experience as inferior to mine because of his toxicity. The reality is that everyone's experience is valid for their life's path. Both of our paths brought us together, and it helped me find a path toward healing. I can't say what our union did for his journey, but I can now see clearly what it did for mine. Although my codependency formed as a behavioral pattern long before I met him, he was the proverbial straw that broke the camel's back. He was what finally pushed me to the brink and made me seek the help I needed to heal. That's the valuable gift my husband brought into my life, illustrating how every person—good or bad—who enters our lives can still bring us something of value to learn from. Your task is to see beyond the haze created by your conditioned mind, allowing yourself to recognize and embrace the gift that each person brings into your life. Additionally, although they may cause you anxiety, it is often that discomfort that is the impetus for real change. If you're comfortable, it's easy to settle into your current situation rather than face the uncertainty of change. When you find yourself under immense pressure and experiencing pain, it often becomes a catalyst for taking action, and it is during these moments that true transformation and change can occur. But those old, toxic relationships often haunt us for years to come. So how do we go about resolving them?

What is the Legacy of Your Toxic Relationships?

Toxic relationships are those that cause harm to one or both partners, either physically, emotionally, mentally, or financially. They are characterized by a lack of trust, respect, communication, and support. My relationship with my mother was toxic, as was my relationship with many romantic partners as an adult. I was looking to please people who were only looking to exploit me. Each person had their own history of trauma that caused them to behave the ways they did. Challenging as it may be to acknowledge, even those who have caused us harm or behaved in toxic ways have their own unique journey to navigate and lessons to learn. Their experience is no less valid than mine, but that doesn't mean I have to endure the effects of their toxicity.

Toxic relationships can affect you in many ways, such as:

1. **Lowering your self-esteem and confidence:** During such times, it's common to question your self-worth and capabilities, experiencing feelings of guilt or shame. Your enthusiasm for hobbies, goals, and passions may wane as well.
2. **Damaging your mental and physical health:** These challenges can manifest in various ways, including increased stress, anxiety, depression, insomnia, headaches, and other physical or emotional symptoms. It's not uncommon to neglect your basic needs, such as proper nutrition, exercise, and sufficient sleep, during this time.
3. **Isolating you from your friends and family:** During this time, it's common to feel some loneliness and disconnection from your social network. You may find yourself avoiding or limiting contact with others, either due to your partner's jealousy, control, or manipulation, or because of your own fear of judgment or criticism.
4. **Impairing your performance and productivity:** The overwhelming stress from the toxic relationship may lead to difficulty concentrating, making decisions, or completing tasks at work, school, or home. Consequently, you might find yourself missing deadlines, skipping classes, or taking more sick days than usual.
5. **Preventing you from growing and learning:** You may stop pursuing new opportunities, challenges, or experiences that could enrich your life. You may also lose sight of your values, beliefs, and dreams.

While toxic relationships can leave lasting scars: it's important to remember that healing is possible. By acknowledging the lessons they bring and allowing yourself to receive their gifts, you can gradually move toward healthier and happier relationships. The journey to healing may take time, but with self-reflection, support, and self-care, you can create a brighter future for yourself. But to do so, you should understand how to interact with other people. Transactional analysis is a theory that views interactions as transactions, and it provides a framework for analyzing and understanding human behavior within these transactions.

Transactional Analysis: Where It Is Usually Depends on Where You Started

An individual's attachment style and experiences during psychosocial development play a significant role in shaping their psychological well-being and can contribute to various psychological disorders, including codependency. Furthermore, these factors can impact one's emotions, thoughts, and behaviors when engaging with others. When interacting with other people, the person who begins the interaction would give what is referred to as the "transaction stimulus," and then you would give what's known as the "transaction response." Psychoanalyst, Eric Berne, studied these transactions in the late 1950s. He based his analysis on Sigmund Freud's theories about how childhood experiences have a significant impact on our adult lives. In fact, those experiences, as we've seen, form the basis for how our personalities develop. Specifically, with regard to transaction analysis, how we were parented can affect the development of our three ego states: Parent, Adult, and Child.

What Berne's research demonstrated is that dysfunctional behavior in adulthood can be the result of self-limiting decisions made in childhood. Our past decisions were made out of a necessity for survival, as they were responses to the challenges we faced during our childhood. As children, we did our best to cope with those crises, and while these coping mechanisms were effective at the time, they may not be suitable for us as adults. These dysfunctional coping patterns become ingrained and create what Berne termed a "life script." He conceived of that as a pre-conscious life plan that affects how our lives play out. Changing the ineffective script and replacing it with mature coping mechanisms is the aim of transactional analysis psychotherapy, which requires a better understanding of the three "ego states." Each state is an entire system of thought, feeling, and behavior that forms the basis of how we interact with each other. Let's examine the three ego states a little more closely.

Child Ego State

The child ego state is activated when we respond to others based on the internal emotions that were conditioned in us during our childhood. In essence, we're reverting back to a time when we were children and felt the same way. Everyone, to some degree, reverts to this state when around their parents or primary childhood caregivers. The child state consists of two subdivisions: the adapted child and the free child.

The adapted child is the ego state that seeks to conform to the wishes of others so our actions please them. We want to be seen as good, and we want to be liked. This actually has very long evolutionary roots, since not being liked could have resulted in ostracization, which, in our ancestors, was a death sentence. Even so, the adapted child has a rebellious side. It causes us to respond with emotional reactivity, resistance, and even hostility in the face of conflict. The free child state is that side of each of us that is creative, spontaneous, playful, and pleasure-seeking. Your individual child ego state is shaped by the reinforcements and experiences you received during your childhood. They can be either positive or negative, but these childhood experiences shape your behavior in certain situations and continue to influence your interactions today.

Parent Ego State

This state also has two subdivisions: the critical/controlling parent and the nurturing parent. In both cases, we learn our parent state from our parents and other authority figures. Berne argued that it is our experiences in the first five years of our life that form the parent ego state. This state of mind is where you form judgments about how someone should or shouldn't be or what they should or shouldn't do. When you're reactive to a situation and simply act from a place of conditioned responses, you're in the parent ego state. Basically, you copy what your parents or other authority figures did rather than analyze the situation from a fresh perspective. This is also known as the "Don't run with a sharp stick, you'll put your eye out" state of conditioning. When interacting from the parent ego state, you may use an authoritative voice, and if you're in the critical parent state, you might express disapproval in harsh and sometimes aggressive ways. If you're in the nurturing parent ego state, you are looking at the situation from a protective perspective. You're trying to soothe someone, but sometimes that can be done inappropriately.

Adult Ego State

This state doesn't have any subdivisions; it is the egoic state where you interact with other people and your environment in the present moment. Essentially, you're in the here and now rather than responding from past conditioning. This is an open, more rational, and less judgmental state. Interactions will likely be more respectful and open to compromise, and you will listen more carefully to others, usually resulting in healthier social interactions.

Your ego state during any given interaction depends on several factors—one of these is how you were conditioned to act or react as a child. If you experienced childhood trauma, it can influence the ego state you find yourself in when triggered by similar circumstances, actions, or words. Often, those past traumas cause us to default subconsciously to either the parent ego state or the child ego state, which are the simplest and fastest reaction states because we don't think about them. We essentially react from a conditioned state. To bring ourselves into the adult ego state, we have to *think* about it. We have to bring ourselves into the present and think about the situation we're in before interacting.

Berne noticed that people need what he referred to as *units of interpersonal recognition* to survive and thrive. Basically, you need your props, and your strokes. People have the capacity to provide either positive or negative feedback, which are referred to as "strokes" in transactional analysis. Recognizing and changing unhealthy patterns of strokes is crucial in helping individuals address conditioned responses and develop a more adult ego state when engaging with others. The objective is to facilitate effective adult communication by encouraging both parties to engage from an adult ego state, promoting healthy and constructive interactions while fostering understanding, empathy, and mutual respect.

My background was one of a very critical mother, and because of that, my conditioned parent ego state is quite judgmental. Frequently, my response to aggressive interactions stemmed from a conditioned child ego state, leading me to react in familiar patterns. The conditioning was so strong, in fact, that bringing myself back into an adult ego state was extremely challenging. This is true of many codependents—they've been conditioned to put their own needs aside to focus on pleasing other people.

Characteristics of Unhealthy Transactions

Toxic relationships are usually characterized by unhealthy interpersonal transactions—so resolving your transactional behaviors would be key to resolving your old, toxic relationships. Unhealthy interpersonal transactions are interactions that harm the well-being of one or both parties involved. They can take various forms, such as manipulation, abuse, neglect, exploitation, or violence. Some characteristics of unhealthy interpersonal transactions include:

1. **Lack of respect:** One or both parties do not value the other's feelings, opinions, boundaries, or rights. They may disregard, criticize, insult, or mock the other person.
2. **Lack of trust:** One or both parties do not believe in the other's honesty, integrity, or reliability. They may doubt, accuse, lie to, or betray the other person.
3. **Lack of communication:** One or both parties do not express their needs, feelings, or expectations clearly and openly. They may avoid, ignore, withhold, or distort information from the other person.
4. **Lack of reciprocity:** One or both parties do not give and take equally in the relationship. They may demand, expect, or take more than they offer, contribute, or share with the other person.
5. **Lack of support:** One or both parties do not provide emotional, practical, or financial assistance to the other when needed. They may neglect, reject, or undermine the other person's goals, interests, or well-being.

Unhealthy interpersonal transactions can have negative consequences for both parties involved. They can damage their self-esteem, mental health, physical health, and social relationships. Therefore, it is important to recognize and avoid unhealthy interpersonal transactions and seek help if needed.

Transactional Analysis and Codependency

Codependent people are those who depend excessively on others for their emotional needs, often sacrificing their own well-being and identity to do so. Codependent individuals often engage in dysfunctional transactions with others, where their ego states are incongruent or mismatched. For instance, a codependent person may assume a child role, seeking validation from a partner who adopts a parent role. Alternatively, a codependent person may take on a parent role, attempting to control or rescue a partner who behaves as a child. These transactions result in power imbalances and hinder the authentic expression of emotions and needs for both individuals involved.

Codependent people also tend to have distorted perceptions of themselves and others, which can affect their transactions. They may have low self-esteem and feel unworthy of love and respect, or they may have unrealistic expectations and demands of others. They may also deny or ignore their own feelings and needs or project them onto others. These perceptions lead to unhealthy patterns of communication and behavior, such as manipulation, guilt-tripping, blaming, passive-aggressiveness, avoidance, or withdrawal. Codependent people can benefit from transactional analysis therapy, which aims to help them identify and change their dysfunctional transactions and perceptions. Through increased self-awareness of their ego states and their impact on interpersonal interactions, individuals can acquire valuable skills in effective and assertive communication. By acknowledging and validating their own emotions and needs, they can prioritize self-care and establish internal boundaries. Furthermore, by cultivating a balanced and realistic perception of themselves and others, they can foster healthier and more fulfilling relationships.

Setting Appropriate Internal Boundaries to Improve Transactions

Setting internal boundaries is a crucial skill for anyone who wants to improve their interpersonal transactions—particularly for codependent people. Internal boundaries are the limits and expectations that we set for ourselves and others in our personal and professional relationships. They help us communicate clearly, respect our own and others' needs and preferences, and avoid unnecessary conflict and misunderstandings. Setting internal boundaries can improve interpersonal transactions in three ways: by enhancing self-awareness, fostering mutual respect, and promoting healthy collaboration.

1. **Increase Self-Awareness:** Setting internal boundaries can enhance self-awareness, which is the foundation of any successful interpersonal transaction. Self-awareness is the ability to recognize and understand one's own emotions, thoughts, values, strengths, weaknesses, and motivations. Setting internal boundaries helps us understand our wants, needs, and limitations. It allows us to recognize triggers and challenges in different situations, promoting self-awareness and healthy interactions with others. This can help us to avoid projecting our issues onto others, take responsibility for our own actions and reactions, and express ourselves authentically and confidently.
2. **Foster Mutual Respect:** Setting internal boundaries can foster mutual respect, which is the key to any harmonious interpersonal transaction. Mutual respect involves acknowledging and valuing the inherent worth, uniqueness, and dignity of both ourselves and others. Setting internal boundaries allows us to respect ourselves by honoring our feelings, opinions, and choices, and by asserting ourselves when necessary. We can also show respect for others by

listening to their perspectives, acknowledging their feelings, and honoring their boundaries. This can help us build trust, rapport, and understanding with others while avoiding conflict and resentment.

3. **Promote Healthy Collaboration:** Setting internal boundaries can promote healthy collaboration, which is the goal of any productive interpersonal transaction. Setting internal boundaries facilitates healthy collaboration by clarifying roles and responsibilities, effective communication of expectations and feedback, and respecting diversity and creativity, enabling individuals to work together toward a common purpose or goal in a mutually beneficial manner. This can then help us achieve our objectives more efficiently, learn from each other's experiences and insights, and celebrate our achievements together. Setting internal boundaries enhances self-awareness, fosters mutual respect, and promotes healthy collaboration, resulting in more enriching personal and professional relationships.

4. We talked about setting boundaries in the previous chapter, and while the exercise in that chapter can help you set your boundaries, internal boundaries are all about you respecting yourself. Just like you wouldn't allow someone else to devalue you, you can't accept devaluation from your inner critic. If you devalue yourself, you won't even recognize the devaluation someone else uses against you as abusive. It is so—whether it comes from you or anyone else. Before you can resolve your old, toxic relationships, you must first value yourself enough to practice self-compassion, self-forgiveness, and true self-love.

Exercise #7

Resolution

Resolution involves a bit more work to heal thoroughly, so this exercise is in three parts. First, it's important to recognize the transactional nature of the toxic relationship and understand the reasons behind your feelings of trauma. Next, you can work toward implementing healthier and more positive forms of interpersonal transactions. By doing so, you can begin the healing process and address the wounds from the past. Let's start with identifying the problem.

Part 1

Identification

One way to practice using internal boundaries is to identify a situation where you felt angry, or resentful toward someone else. It could be a family member, friend, coworker, or anyone else. Write down what happened, how you felt, and what you did or said in response. Then, reflect on the following questions:

- What boundary was crossed or violated by the other person?
- How did you express your boundary to them? Was it clear and assertive or vague and passive?
- How did they react to your boundary? Did they respect, ignore, or challenge it?
- How did you feel after the interaction? Relieved, guilty, frustrated, or something else?
- What could you do differently next time to set and maintain a healthier internal boundary?

This exercise can help you become more aware of your own internal boundaries and how they affect your interpersonal transactions. It can also help you improve your skills in setting and communicating your boundaries to others respectfully and effectively.

Part 2

Implementation

Think again about the situation you identified in Part 1 of this exercise. Think about what triggered your negative emotions and what you wanted to say or do at that moment. Then, write down three possible responses that you could have given using internal boundaries. For example:

- **Situation**: Your boss asks you to work overtime on a project that is not your responsibility.
- **Trigger**: You feel overworked, unappreciated, and taken advantage of.
- **Possible responses**:

❖ "I'm sorry, but I can't work overtime on this project. It's not part of my job description and I have other priorities to attend to."

❖ "I appreciate your confidence in me, but I'm not available to work overtime on this project. It's outside my scope of work, and I have other commitments that I need to honor."

❖ "No, thank you. I'm not interested in working overtime on this project. It's not aligned with my goals and values, and I have other plans for my time."

Try to use assertive language, and express your feelings and needs clearly—while respecting the other person's feelings and needs as well. Avoid blaming, criticizing, or judging the other person or agreeing to something that you don't want to do. Remember that you have the right to say no, and that you are responsible for your own happiness and well-being.

Part 3

Healing Old Toxic Relationships

One way to heal old, toxic relationships is to improve your interpersonal transactions. Interpersonal transactions are the exchanges of words, gestures, and emotions that happen between two or more people. They can be positive, negative, or neutral. In this exercise, you will learn how to identify and change your interpersonal transactions to make them more positive and constructive.

- **Consider the Relationship You Want to Heal:** Think of an old, toxic relationship that you want to heal. It can be with a family member, friend, colleague, or anyone else. Write down the name of the person and the reason why the relationship is toxic.
- **Recall Your Transactional Style with Them:** Recall some interpersonal transactions that you had with that person in the past. Write down at least three examples of what you said or did, and how the person reacted. Try to be as specific and honest as possible.
- **Analysis:** Analyze each interpersonal transaction that you wrote down. Use the following questions to guide you:

❖ Was the transaction positive, negative, or neutral?
❖ How did it affect your and the other person's feelings?
❖ What was the underlying message or intention behind the transaction?
❖ How could you have said or done something different to make the transaction more positive?

Write down your answers for each transaction.

1. **Practice, Practice, Practice:** Practice changing your interpersonal transactions with that person. Imagine that you have a chance to talk to them again and write down what you

would say or do differently using the insights from your analysis. Try to use positive words, gestures, and emotions that show respect, and empathy.
2. **How Can It Help?:** Reflect on how changing your interpersonal transactions can help you heal the old, toxic relationship. Write down how you feel after doing this exercise. Do you feel more hopeful, confident, or relieved? Do you think the other person would respond differently if you used these new transactions? Can you see their point of view with compassion? How would that affect your relationship?

This exercise can help you improve your interpersonal transactions and heal old, toxic relationships. By changing your words, gestures, and emotions, you can create more positive and constructive exchanges with others. This can lead to more trust and harmony in your relationships. It can also help you better understand what exactly was wrong the first time around. You can foster compassion toward both the person and their behavioral style, while also showing compassion toward yourself and your own reactions. This compassionate perspective can aid in overcoming the lingering effects of the toxic relationship, as it allows you to gain insight into what went wrong and how you would approach things differently now.

As a final note, this exercise can help with writing a letter to the person involved in the toxic relationship. Through personal growth and reflection, you can gain a deeper understanding of the motivations behind the actions of both yourself and the other person in the toxic relationship. This understanding allows you to recognize the underlying reasons for their behavior and your own reactions; it brings clarity to the dynamics of the relationship and enables you to make sense of the past. You can offer them your forgiveness, whether or not you ever want them in your life again. You can send the letter to them or not as well; it doesn't matter. What matters is that you've expressed yourself and processed those emotions.

Final Thoughts on Resolving Old, Toxic Relationships

Healing those old, unhealthy relationships is vital for moving forward. If you don't do this work, you will dwell on them, even if only in your subconscious mind. When you resolve them, then can you truly let go of your past and move forward with your future. You're free from the prison the toxicity created in your mind. Your past becomes merely a series of events that happened to you as opposed to an integral part of your identity. Through the process of self-reflection and personal growth, you can come to the realization that you deserve better treatment and that you played a role in allowing the toxic relationship to persist. This realization empowers you to take responsibility for your own well-being and make choices that align with your self-worth and self-respect. You can fully understand the problem, see it in a compassionate light, and cultivate forgiveness for both your abusers and yourself. Whether or not they ever change, apologize, or even understand the wounds they inflicted is of no consequence. What matters is that you see it, and you've let it go. Now, you can truly seek the road to a happier life.

Chapter 8

The Road to a Happier You

Healing from codependency can be likened to receiving a "get out of jail" free card, where you experience the liberation of a prisoner who has been proven innocent. It marks the start of a transformative journey, fostering a fresh and profound connection with yourself. Furthermore, it paves the way for renewed relationships with those around you, allowing for healthier dynamics and interactions. Make no mistake; there may be some people who have grown accustomed to the old, people-pleasing version of you and might be taken aback by the changes in your behavior. Those are the people you might choose to say goodbye to as you forge a new path for yourself. But freeing yourself from the chains of codependency is just the first step in the journey. You'll find there are other wounds you'll have to heal along the way too. The wounds that created your codependency likely left other scars as well. It's crucial to dedicate time to heal those aspects of yourself. Additionally, it's important to acknowledge that even after healing, you may encounter a range of emotions, including some that might catch you by surprise. You've been living a certain way for a long time now, and it's all about to change, so how do you go forward, and what other challenges might you encounter?

What Emotions Will You Notice?

Healing from codependency involves recognizing and changing unhealthy patterns of behavior and developing a sense of self-worth, autonomy, and assertiveness. It also involves learning to prioritize your own needs and feelings and set healthy limits with others. Healing from codependency can be a challenging and rewarding process, and it can evoke a range of emotions along the way. All reactions are valid, and it's essential to be prepared for the variety of emotions you may experience.

Some emotions you might feel once you've healed your codependent patterns include:

1. **Relief:** You may feel relieved that you no longer have to carry the burden of someone else's issues or endure their abuse or manipulation. You may feel free from the stress and anxiety that plagued you in your codependent relationship. It may also be comforting to know that you can finally focus on yourself and your own goals without feeling guilty or selfish.
2. **Joy:** Discovering new aspects of yourself, your interests, and your passions can evoke a sense of joy. Cultivating healthy relationships built on mutual respect, trust, and support can bring forth feelings of elation, and recognizing your worthiness of love and happiness and embracing the power to create a fulfilling life may fill you with delight.
3. **Anger:** Reflecting on how your codependent relationship harmed you or how the other person took advantage of you can evoke feelings of anger. Recognizing the injustice and unfairness of what you endured may also ignite anger within you. Additionally, confronting the underlying causes of your codependency, such as childhood trauma or family dysfunction, may stir up anger. It is important to remember that anger can be a healthy and empowering emotion, as long

as you express it constructively and prevent it from overwhelming you.

4. **Grief:** Experiencing grief is natural as you navigate the aftermath of your codependent relationship and the person you were during that time. It is normal to mourn the loss of the relationship and the accompanying hopes and dreams you had. Letting go of the fantasy of what could have been and accepting the reality of your situation may also evoke feelings of grief. While grief can be painful, it is an important emotion that allows you to process your loss and embark on the journey of moving forward.

5. **Pride:** Recognizing your progress and growth in your healing journey can evoke feelings of pride. You may take pride in celebrating your achievements and accomplishments, regardless of their size. Embracing your strengths, talents, and inherent value can also generate a sense of pride. It is important to channel this emotion in a positive and motivating way, avoiding the pitfalls of arrogance or complacency. Pride can serve as a reminder of your resilience and serve as a catalyst for further personal growth.

6. **Depression:** You may also feel some level of depression while orienting yourself to the possibilities in your life now. Although you're no longer carrying the burden of someone else's needs and desires, you may feel uncertain about the path your life will take now. You may wonder what your purpose is if you are no longer serving someone else. This does not mean that the healing has not been effective. It's something to expect as you define the direction your life will take now that you're finally free.

There is nothing wrong with anything you might feel, but you might not expect to experience negative emotions. Emotional fluctuations are normal during the healing process, and it's important to realize that codependency may not be the only behavioral pattern you've picked up through the years. Let's take a look at some of the other patterns you might have developed.

What Other Behavioral Patterns are Common in Codependents?

As codependency developed, it is likely that you also adopted other ingrained patterns of behavior. Here are some common ones that may be part and parcel of your codependency.

1. **Confluence:** This is when a person loses their sense of individuality and merges with others or the environment. They may avoid conflict and try to please everyone. They may also have difficulty expressing their feelings and opinions.
2. **Introjection:** This is when a person passively accepts the values and attitudes of others without questioning or evaluating them. They may internalize the expectations of others and try to live up to them. They may also have low self-esteem and lack of autonomy. Introjected beliefs can be like a ghost fluttering around in the halls of your mind, whispering certain judgmental concepts in your ear. It can affect your behavior on a subliminal level, and it is very difficult to recognize.
3. **Projection:** This is when a person denies or rejects an aspect of themselves and attributes it to someone else. They may see in others what they do not want to see in themselves. They may also blame others for their own problems or criticize others for their own faults. When this happens, you know it's part of your shadow, and although you may have addressed other shadows, each time you encounter one, it's important to welcome that part of yourself into the light as well.

4. **Retroflection:** This is when a person turns their actions or feelings back onto themselves instead of expressing them outwardly. They may do to themselves what they want to do to others or what they want others to do to them. They may also suppress their anger or hurt and harm themselves instead. This is another very common pattern in codependents. Our entire self-value is based on what we can do for others, and we fall all over ourselves trying not to hurt them, no matter how much we might be hurting ourselves.
5. **Deflection:** This is when a person avoids direct contact or communication with themselves or others. They may distract themselves from their own feelings or issues by changing the subject, making jokes, or being vague. They may also avoid intimacy or commitment by keeping a distance from others. You might feel this for a while out of fear that you will fall back into a pattern of codependency. But distraction and avoidance is never the answer; self-respect and self-compassion is the way.
6. **Proflexion:** This is when a person anticipates future events or outcomes and reacts to them as if they were already happening. They may worry excessively about what might go wrong or what others might think of them. They may also miss out on the present by living in the future. As a codependent, I did this all the time to avoid negative feedback from others in my life. It's also a common pattern among people who want to have a plan for every possible outcome. They don't want life to surprise them, and they try to anticipate everything that might happen.
7. **Egotism:** This is when a person has an exaggerated sense of self-importance and superiority over others. They may believe they are always right and their needs and opinions are more valuable than those of others. They may also lack empathy or compassion for others and exploit them for their own benefit. Once you've freed yourself of codependence, it

can be easy for the pendulum to swing too far to the other side. You may go overboard in valuing your own needs to the point of becoming egotistic.

Understanding these patterns can help you become more aware of your own behavior and make positive changes if needed or avoid pitfalls after you've healed. It's important to address any other negative patterns you might have developed alongside your codependency as well. Unfortunately, for complicated conditions like this, there are often a number of other habits we've fallen into; now that you've developed a heightened sense of self-awareness, you're much better equipped to recognize unproductive behavioral strategies and make positive changes. By doing so, you set yourself up for success in discovering your life's purpose and making strides toward accomplishing your goals. But how do you go about that?

How Do You Identify Your Life's Purpose?

Finding your life's purpose can be a challenging albeit rewarding journey. It can help you feel more fulfilled, motivated, and aligned with your values. But how do you discover what your purpose is? Here are some steps you can take to explore your passions, talents, and goals.

1. **Reflect on your strengths and interests**: What are you good at? What do you enjoy doing? What makes you feel alive and energized? These can serve as indicators or hints toward your life's purpose. You might also ask yourself what you love to do, even if you're not being paid to do it. Can you turn that into something that can fulfill your desires in life? You'll want to think about this creatively. For instance, if you have a passion for painting but recognize the challenges of making a sustainable income as an artist, you may need to explore alternative career paths that can provide financial stability for yourself and your dependents. Is there another way you could work as an artist without relying

solely on selling your paintings? You could teach art classes or work in an arts and crafts store. There isn't just one way to create a life that fulfills your purpose.

2. **Experiment with different activities and experiences:** Try new things that spark your curiosity or challenge you to grow. You might find something that resonates with you or reveals a hidden potential. Perhaps you love nature and being out in the natural world. Join a hiking club and see if being out regularly in nature is something that continues to make you feel fulfilled. Then you can explore ways you might turn that into a career. You might also volunteer doing something that interests you to see if it's a lasting interest or just a passing fad.

3. **Seek feedback and guidance:** Talk to people who know you well or who have similar interests. Ask them what they think your purpose is or how they found theirs—you might get some valuable insights or inspiration from doing so. Sometimes, the people we are closest to see things in us that we don't realize are there. Sometimes, we are too close to ourselves to evaluate our strengths and weaknesses objectively or recognize our true talents and abilities.

4. **Align your purpose with your values and vision:** Think about what matters most to you and what kind of impact you want to have in the world. How does your purpose fit with these aspirations? How can you use your purpose to serve others and make a difference? You might even write your own obituary. It may sound morbid at first, but what is it you want it to say? In contemplating our lives, our hope is that others will acknowledge the significance of our actions, the positive transformations we've facilitated, and the meaningful bonds we've forged. We aspire to be remembered for making a difference, inspiring joy, and leaving a lasting legacy of love and positivity. This can help you determine your purpose in life.

Once you believe you've identified your purpose in life, you'll likely need to identify a set of goals to achieve that potential fully. That's the next step in creating your happiest life.

How Do You Set Appropriate Goals?

Once you've freed yourself from that unwanted responsibility of other people's happiness, it's time to focus on your own. This means identifying and setting goals. Goals help us to clarify our vision, focus our efforts, and measure our progress. However, not all goals are created equal. Some goals may be too vague, unrealistic, or irrelevant to our true needs and aspirations. How can we identify and set goals that are reasonable and achievable? Here are some tips to guide you.

Use the SMART Criteria

SMART stands for Specific, Measurable, Achievable, Relevant, and Time-bound. A SMART goal is clear, concrete, realistic, aligned with your values and priorities, and has a deadline. For example, instead of saying "I want to lose weight," a SMART goal would be "I want to lose 10 pounds in three months by following a healthy diet and exercising three times a week." Now that you're focusing on what you want to achieve in life, you can list what you'll need to do to achieve that goal. For instance, if you want to lose that 10 pounds, you'll first need to determine what kind of diet plan you'll follow, get the food in the house, eliminate other types of food from the house, determine an exercise routine, get a scale, and set a start date. These then become milestones you'll need to meet on the journey toward your goal. Similarly, if you decide you want to pursue a new career, you might need to get the appropriate education, and to do that, you should determine which school to go to, apply to that school, and secure the funding to pay for it.

The path to achieving your goal may appear overwhelming at times, but by breaking it down into smaller, attainable milestones, you can make it much more manageable. You can also think of it this way—the time is going to pass whether you're working toward your goal or not, so you might as well be working toward something that will ultimately bring you fulfillment and make you happy.

Break It Down

To overcome the overwhelming feeling of a daunting goal, we can break it down into smaller, more manageable steps that are more attainable and within reach. As in the example above, you would make a list of the steps you'll need to take to achieve your goal. Then, you can establish a timeline for accomplishing each step, ensuring that you progress steadily toward your goal within a structured timeframe.

When I made the decision to pursue a degree in psychology, there were several steps I needed to take. First, I had to research and choose the schools I wanted to apply to. Then, I completed the application process for each school, ensuring that I met all the requirements. Next, I focused on securing the necessary funding to cover the expenses associated with my education. Additionally, I had to plan and organize the logistics of relocating to the area where the school was located, including finding suitable housing. Alongside these practical considerations, I also had to plan my course schedule carefully and acquire the necessary materials for each class. These were just some of the many steps involved in pursuing my goal of obtaining a degree in psychology. That's a lot, but you can set a timetable for each part. It works really well, for example, to break down the steps in the process into daily, weekly, monthly, and yearly milestones. To effectively manage your goals and stay organized, it's helpful to establish a regular routine for reviewing and planning. On a daily basis, take time to review and outline the tasks and objectives you aim to accomplish for that day.

Each week, dedicate a day to assess your progress, set targets, and plan for the upcoming week. Similarly, on a monthly basis, take the opportunity to plan for the next while reflecting on your achievements from the previous. Lastly, on an annual basis, set overarching goals for the upcoming year and reflect on your accomplishments and growth from the past year. By implementing these regular review and planning sessions, you can stay focused, motivated, and on track toward achieving your goals. Treat it like you're the CEO of your business, which is working toward achieving your happiest life. Use a daily, weekly, and monthly planner to set your milestones and schedule meetings to review your progress and plan for what comes next. You're much more likely to stick to this process if you formalize it. Making plans like this also gives you a material list that you can check off each time you complete a milestone. This is a very satisfying feeling.

Adapt Milestones and Goals as Necessary

Our goals are not set in stone. They can change over time as we learn new information, face new challenges, or discover new opportunities. Therefore, it is important to review and adjust your goals regularly to make sure they are still relevant and realistic. You can use feedback from others, self-reflection, or performance indicators to evaluate your progress and identify areas that need improvement. This is the benefit of the planner. As you conduct meetings with yourself, you can review your milestones and goals to see if you are still excited to complete them. If something has changed, you can make the necessary adjustments. For example, while pursuing my degree in psychology, I initially had the goal of obtaining a general psychology degree. However, as I progressed in my education and explored various areas within psychology, my interests evolved, leading me to adjust my focus and explore different specializations and career paths. This flexibility allowed me to align my studies and future goals with my evolving passions and interests in the field of psychology. Even minor goals like losing that 10 pounds in three months might change later. You might discover weightlifting as a passion, but instead of just losing weight, your focus may shift toward becoming more muscular and toned. Muscle weighs more than fat, so while you may not see a significant decrease in overall weight as originally anticipated, the weight you retain or even gain is attributed to the healthier composition of muscle, resulting in a more aesthetically pleasing and toned physique.

Celebrate!

Celebrate your achievements and learn from your failures. Setting and achieving goals is not a linear process; there will be ups and downs along the way, and it is important to celebrate your achievements and reward yourself for your hard work. When you achieve a milestone along the way, determine some kind of reward you will give yourself. It can be as simple as treating yourself to a meal at your favorite restaurant or taking a well-deserved day off to relax and unwind. Whatever form it takes, make sure to allocate time to reward yourself for each milestone achieved. This is also a good time to express your gratitude for what you have accomplished and have now; doing so can boost your motivation and confidence. At the same time, it is also important to learn from your failures and mistakes. This will help you overcome obstacles and grow from your experiences. When you make a mistake or experience a failure, reflect on what happened that didn't work, and write down what you could have done better to prevent that from happening. This way, you can avoid making the same mistakes over and over again.

By following these tips, you can start moving forward toward your best life. It really doesn't matter how long it takes to reach your overall goal; what matters is that you're focusing on your goals, dreams, and happiness. By taking intentional action and making conscious choices, you have the power to shape your life according to your desires. This proactive approach is also essential in building healthy, supportive, and mutually respectful relationships with others.

Exercise #8

Your Happy Life

As the CEO of Happier You, Inc., your job is to lay out the company's (your) goals that are in line with your values and set an agenda for achieving those goals. This two-part exercise will help you do just that. We'll start with identifying the goals, and then move on to the agenda.

Part 1

Identify Your Goals

One of the most important steps in personal development is identifying the goals that are in line with your life purpose. This exercise will help you to clarify what you want to achieve and why.

1. **Write down your life purpose statement:** This is a sentence that summarizes what you believe is the meaning of your existence and what you want to contribute to the world.
2. **Brainstorm a list of possible goals that are related to your life purpose:** These can be short-term or long-term, personal or professional, specific or general.
3. **Evaluate each goal using the SMART criteria:** Specific, Measurable, Achievable, Relevant, and Time-bound. Make sure each goal is clear, realistic, and aligned with your life purpose.
4. **Prioritize your goals based on their importance and urgency:** You can use a matrix to rank them according to four categories: Important and Urgent, Important but Not

Urgent, Not Important but Urgent, and Not Important and Not Urgent.
5. **Create a timeline:** Choose one or two goals from each category that you want to focus on for the next week, month, quarter, or year. Write down an action plan for each goal, detailing the steps you need to take, the resources you need, and any deadlines.
6. **Review your goals and action plans regularly:** Track your progress and celebrate your achievements. Adjust your goals and plans as needed based on your feedback and changing circumstances.

Part 2

Create Your Agenda

The next step after creating your goals and laying out a timeline is to organize your agenda. You want to have daily time for reflection and planning, a weekly meeting for organizing and reviewing, a monthly meeting for laying out the next month's agenda and assessing your progress, and a yearly meeting to chart your progress and plan for the next year's agenda. You're much more likely to be successful in following an agenda if you stay consistent in your time. For each of the prompts below, lay out a plan for your company's meetings.

1. Every day at _____ AM/PM, I will take _____ minutes to practice mindfulness around the day's goals, review the previous day's progress, and plan for the current day.
2. On _____ (Choose a day of the week), I will take _____ (hour/hours) at _____ AM/PM to plan for the upcoming week and review the progress made in the previous week.

234

3. On _____ (DATE), I will meet for _____ (length of time) to review the previous month's progress and plan the next month's agenda.
4. On _____ (DATE), I will meet for _____ (length of time) to review the previous year's accomplishments and set the agenda for the upcoming year.

Once you've laid out your agenda, you can now put the dates and times into your calendar and set reminders as appropriate. It's also important to build self-care time into your agenda, and you might consider planning for that in a similar manner.

Final Thoughts on Your Road to Happiness

As a recovering codependent, embarking on the journey of discovering your life's purpose and setting meaningful goals is a significant stride away from the negative behavioral patterns associated with codependency. It signifies your commitment to personal growth and cultivating a healthier and more fulfilling life. You're now working toward your own happiness and success, and that's a huge change for the better. As you continue to grow in confidence and satisfaction, you'll be even more motivated to keep going, and you'll also have much more to be grateful for when you celebrate your achievements. To help fulfill your goals, we'll talk in the next chapter about implementing new habits as you move forward with your new life.

Chapter 9

New Habits, New Life

Now that you have liberated yourself from codependency and defined the goals you wish to pursue in your life, there are numerous new, healthier habits and strategies that you can adopt as you move forward. These practices will support your personal growth and contribute to a more fulfilling and balanced life. For me, this involved prioritizing my self-care, regardless of everything else going on in my life. I suspect that's true for many codependents. I had a bad habit of not attending to my own needs if any other part of my life stressed me out. The problem with that is that there's always something stressful happening at any given time in your life. I used to believe that I would find the time to prioritize self-care when I had less stress in my life, but the truth is, I was constantly feeling overwhelmed and stressed. What's more, the self-care activities I needed to prioritize were those that would help to alleviate my stress.

The truth is that life's a challenge, and there will always be something that's stressing you out, even if it's good stress. So you need to make self-care a habit that you prioritize as much as you would eating regularly or brushing your teeth. You also need to make your new coping mechanisms, like learning to listen to intuition or your body, into habits as well. As a codependent, your brain adopted a habit of constantly seeking out problems that other people were experiencing, so you would rush to help them. That was something that helped you survive as a child, but now it's time to take care of yourself. Now, you need to train your brain to use positive self-talk, self-trust, and self-care as mechanisms for reacting to stress, rather than negative, self-punishing ones. So how do you change your habits?

Take Off Your Mask

One of the most influential concepts in psychology is the idea of the persona, developed by Carl Jung. The persona is a mask or role that we present to the world, especially in social situations. It is not our true self, but rather, a compromise between our inner nature and the expectations of society. The persona helps us fit in, conform, and avoid conflict. However, Jung also warned that the persona can become a problem if we identify too much with it and lose touch with our authentic self. Jung defined the persona as "a kind of mask, designed on the one hand to make a definite impression upon others, and on the other to conceal the true nature of the individual." He proposed that each individual possesses a unique psychological makeup, referred to as the individuum. However, this individuum often clashes with societal norms and values, referred to as the collective. Thus, we create a persona to bridge the gap between our individuality and our social roles. The persona is not a fixed or static entity, but instead a flexible and adaptable one. We can change our persona depending on the situation and the audience. For example, we may act differently at work, at home, or with friends.

The persona is not necessarily a bad thing. In fact, Jung considered it as a necessary and useful function of the psyche. It allows us to communicate and cooperate with others, express ourselves in appropriate ways, and protect ourselves from criticism or rejection. It also helps us achieve our goals and aspirations. Without a persona, we would be exposed and vulnerable, unable to cope with the demands and challenges of life. However, Jung also cautioned that the persona can become a source of psychological problems if we over-identify with it and neglect our true self. He called this phenomenon "inflation of the persona." When this happens, we lose touch with our inner reality and become alienated from ourselves. We may also become rigid and inflexible in our behavior, unable to adapt to changing circumstances or new experiences. We may also develop a false sense of superiority or inferiority, depending on how we compare our persona with others. Moreover, we may suffer from inner conflict and dissatisfaction as we repress or deny aspects of ourselves that do not fit with our persona.

Jung suggested that one way to overcome the inflation of the persona is to take off the masks we put on to cope with life. He advocated for a process called individuation, which involves self-exploration and self-realization. Individuation entails becoming aware of our authentic self and integrating it with our conscious personality. It also involves acknowledging and embracing the aspects of ourselves that we have rejected or disregarded, known as the shadow. By doing so, we can achieve a balance between our inner and outer worlds and our individuum vs the overall collective. Jung's theory of the persona offers valuable insight into how we present ourselves to others and how we can relate to ourselves. You've already done much of the work proposed by Jung as part of taking off your mask. Now, you just need to learn to trust your true self. It resides inside of you, and it is always guiding you toward what is ultimately best for you. As codependents, learning to listen to our intuition is very difficult; we have developed a habit of relying on other people's suggestions as well as their judgments, but now we are on our own. That's a good thing, but listening to yourself and trusting your intuition is still a vital part of that process.

How Can You Learn to Trust Yourself?

Trust is a vital component of any healthy relationship, including the one you have with yourself. Learning to trust yourself can help you overcome self-doubt, fear, and anxiety. It can also boost your confidence, creativity, and happiness. But how can you learn to trust yourself? Here are some tips:

1. **Listen to your intuition:** Your intuition is your inner voice that guides you. It is based on your experiences, values, and feelings. When you listen to your intuition, you are trusting yourself to make good decisions and follow your own path.
2. **Accept your mistakes:** No one is perfect and everyone makes mistakes, so Instead of beating yourself up for your errors, accept them as opportunities to learn and grow. When you accept your mistakes, you are trusting yourself to handle challenges and overcome setbacks.
3. **Celebrate your achievements:** You have accomplished many things in your life, both big and small. Recognize and appreciate your achievements and acknowledge your strengths and talents. When you celebrate your achievements, you are trusting yourself to pursue your goals and dreams.
4. **Seek feedback:** Feedback from others can help you improve your skills, gain new perspectives, and discover new opportunities. Seek feedback from people who support you and want you to succeed. When you seek feedback, you are trusting yourself to be open-minded and adaptable.
5. **Be kind to yourself:** Self-compassion is the practice of treating yourself with kindness, understanding, and forgiveness. It means being supportive of yourself, especially when you are struggling or suffering. When you are kind to yourself, you are trusting yourself to cope with difficulties and heal from pain.

Learning to trust yourself is a process that takes time and effort. But it is worth it because it can transform your life for the better. By following these tips, you can build a strong and positive relationship with yourself.

Why Expressing Gratitude Can Help

Gratitude is a powerful emotion that can improve your well-being, happiness, and success, and it's a powerful way to express trust for yourself and your intuition. First, expressing gratitude can help you appreciate your achievements and recognize your strengths. When you acknowledge how far you have come and how much you have learned, you boost your self-esteem and confidence, and you learn to trust yourself more. You also avoid taking things for granted and becoming complacent. Instead, you feel motivated to keep growing and pursuing your goals. Second, expressing gratitude can enhance your relationships and social support. When you thank others for their help and support, you show them that you value and respect them. You also foster a positive and cooperative atmosphere that encourages mutual trust and understanding. By expressing gratitude, you strengthen your bonds with your family, friends, colleagues, and mentors. Third, expressing gratitude can reduce your stress and increase your resilience. When you focus on the positive aspects of your life and what you have accomplished, you reduce those negative and overwhelming emotions. Additionally, cultivating a more optimistic and hopeful outlook can aid in coping with challenges and setbacks. By expressing gratitude, you can improve your mental and emotional health, ultimately helping you appreciate your achievements, enhance your relationships, and reduce your stress.

Gratitude is feeling appreciation and thankfulness for the benefits and blessings we receive in life. It is a powerful and positive emotion that can enhance our well-being, happiness, and relationships. However, gratitude is not something that comes naturally to everyone; some people may struggle to feel or express gratitude, especially in difficult or stressful situations. How can we practice expressing gratitude more often and more sincerely? Here are some tips and strategies to help you cultivate a habit of gratitude.

1. **Keep a gratitude journal:** A gratitude journal is a simple and effective way to record and reflect on the things you are grateful for every day. You can use a notebook, smartphone app, or any other tool that works for you. The key is to write down at least three things you are grateful for each day, preferably in the morning or before going to bed. Try to be specific and detailed and avoid repeating the same things every day. For example, instead of writing, "I am grateful for my family," you could write, "I am grateful for the hug my daughter gave me this morning" or "I am grateful for the funny joke my brother told me yesterday." Practicing gratitude through writing can help shift your focus toward the positive aspects of life and serve as a reminder of the sources of joy and meaning in your life.
2. **Share gratitude to others:** Sometimes it helps to express that gratitude openly with those around you. You can do this by saying thank you, writing a note, sending a message, giving a compliment, or doing a favor. Expressing gratitude to others can strengthen your relationships, boost your self-esteem, and make others feel valued and appreciated. It can also create a positive feedback loop, where the more you express gratitude, the more you receive it from others. Try to express gratitude to at least one person every day and be genuine and specific in your appreciation. For instance, instead of saying, "Thank you for your help," you could say, "Thank you for taking the time to explain this concept to me" or "Thank you for being such a supportive and caring friend."
3. **Practice gratitude meditation:** Gratitude meditation is a form of mindfulness meditation that involves focusing on the things you are grateful for in the present moment. You can practice gratitude meditation by sitting comfortably, closing your eyes, and taking a few deep breaths. Then, bring to mind something or someone you are grateful for and feel that

gratitude in your body and mind. You can also repeat a mantra or affirmation, such as "I am grateful for..." or "Thank you for..." You can practice gratitude meditation for as long as you like and switch to different objects of gratitude as you wish. Gratitude meditation can help you cultivate a sense of abundance and contentment in your life while reducing stress and negative emotions.

4. **Use gratitude prompts:** Gratitude prompts are questions or statements that stimulate your thinking and help you generate ideas for things you are grateful for. They can be useful when you feel stuck or uninspired in your gratitude practice or when you want to explore new aspects of gratitude and expand your appreciation. You can find gratitude prompts online, in books, or create your own. Some examples of gratitude prompts include:

- What made you smile today?
- What did you learn today?
- What are you looking forward to?
- What have you overcome or achieved recently?
- What do you enjoy doing?
- What do you love about yourself?
- What are you proud of?
- What makes your life easier or more comfortable?
- What inspires you?
- What are you passionate about?

Using gratitude prompts can help you expand your perspective and discover new things to be grateful for.

5. **Make gratitude a part of your routine.** The best way to practice expressing gratitude is to make it a part of your daily life. You can do this by setting reminders, creating rituals, or integrating gratitude into your existing habits. For example, you can:

- Start or end your day with a gratitude journal entry.

- ❖ Say thank you to someone every time you interact with them.
- ❖ Meditate on gratitude every morning or evening.
- ❖ Write a thank-you note every week.
- ❖ Compliment someone every day.
- ❖ Do a random act of kindness every day.
- ❖ Think of three things you are grateful for every time you eat a meal.
- ❖ Review your gratitude journal entries every month.

Making gratitude a part of your routine can help you develop a consistent and sustainable practice of expressing gratitude. Expressing gratitude is not only a polite and courteous gesture (including to yourself) but also a powerful and beneficial practice that can improve your well-being, happiness, and relationships. Most important of all is that it's a powerful way to acknowledge that you trust yourself to recognize your own strengths and weaknesses, seek feedback from others, and use that feedback to improve your life. It's as much about respecting and honoring yourself as it is about thanking other people for helping you.

Healthy Habits to Support the New You

Habits are patterns of behavior that we repeat automatically and often unconsciously. Habit stacking is a technique that can help you implement new, healthy habits into your daily routine. These would include your self-care habits like regular exercise and meditation. Habits can help us save time and energy, but they can also be hard to change or break. According to the habit loop model, habits consist of three components: a cue, a routine, and a reward. A cue is a trigger that initiates a habit, such as a time of day, location, or emotion. A routine is an action that we perform in response to the cue, like brushing our teeth, checking our phone, or eating a snack. A reward is an outcome that we get from the routine, such as a feeling of freshness, satisfaction, or pleasure. The habit loop model suggests that habits are formed through a process of reinforcement and repetition. When we experience a positive reward from a routine, we associate it with the cue and strengthen the habit. The more we repeat the habit loop, the more ingrained it becomes in our brain and behavior. However, habits are not fixed and immutable; they can be modified or replaced by introducing new cues, routines, or rewards. One very effective technique for doing this is habit stacking.

Habit stacking involves linking a new habit to an existing one so that you can trigger the new behavior automatically. For example, if you want to start meditating every morning, you can stack it on top of your existing habit of brushing your teeth. This way, every time you finish brushing your teeth, you can immediately start meditating for a few minutes. Habit stacking has several benefits for creating and maintaining healthy habits. First, it reduces the need for willpower and motivation, since you are using an existing cue to trigger the new habit. Second, it helps you integrate the new habit into your lifestyle rather than adding it as an extra task. Third, it creates a positive feedback loop, as it allows you to feel good about accomplishing both the old and the new habit.

To implement habit stacking effectively, you need to follow some steps. Here are some tips on how to do it:

1. **Identify the new habit you want to create:** Make sure it is specific, measurable, achievable, relevant, and time-bound (SMART). For example, instead of saying, "I want to exercise more," say "I want to do 10 pushups every morning."
2. **Identify the existing habit that you can link the new habit to:** Choose a habit that is stable, consistent, and relevant to the new habit. For example, if you want to do pushups every morning, you can link it to your habit of getting out of bed, drinking a glass of water, brushing your teeth.

3. **Design a clear and simple plan for how to stack the habits:** Use the formula: "After/before I [existing habit], I will [new habit] in/at the [time of day]." For example, "After I drink a glass of water in the morning, I will do 10 pushups."
4. **Write down your plan and put it somewhere visible:** Your mirror is a good place to put it since you look there everyday. This will help you remember your intention and reinforce your commitment. You can also use reminders or alarms on your phone or computer to prompt you to commit to the new habit.
5. **Start small and gradually increase the difficulty or duration of the new habit:** Don't try to do too much at once, as this can overwhelm you and make you give up. Instead, start with a small and easy version of the new habit and gradually make it harder or longer as you get used to it. For example, start with five pushups and increase by one every week until you reach ten.
6. **Track your progress and reward yourself for your achievements:** Use a calendar, journal, or app to record when you do the new habit and how it makes you feel. Celebrate your successes and reward yourself with something that brings you joy and aligns with your goals. For instance, you can treat yourself to a nutritious snack or indulge in watching an episode of your favorite show after completing your pushups.
7. **Review and adjust your plan as needed.** Sometimes, things may not go as planned, and you may encounter challenges or obstacles that hinder your ability to maintain the new habit. Don't get discouraged or give up. Instead, review your plan and see what you can change or improve to make it easier or more enjoyable for you. For instance, if you find it hard to do pushups in the morning, you can try doing them at another time that suits you better, like perhaps at night.

Habit stacking is a powerful tool that can help you create and sustain new, healthy habits in your life. By following these steps, you can make positive changes in your behavior and well-being without relying on willpower or motivation alone. You will also cut down significantly on the amount of time you need to integrate the habit into your routine.

Exercise #9

The Path to a New You

The exercises in this chapter are designed to help you learn to trust yourself and your intuition more. As in previous chapters, there are two parts, which are geared toward helping you trust your intuition and build new habits.

Part 1

Trusting Your Intuition

One way to learn to trust your intuition is to listen to your inner voice and act on it. Here is an exercise you can try:

- Go to your quiet place where you can relax and focus.
- Close your eyes and take a few deep breaths, expanding your belly and chest.
- Think of a question or situation that you need guidance on.
- Ask your intuition for an answer or direction. You can do this silently or out loud.
- Pay attention to any feelings, images, words, or sensations that come to you. Don't judge or analyze them—just observe them.
- Write down what you received from your intuition. It may be clear or vague, but trust that it has meaning for you.

- Decide how you will act on your intuition. You can follow it completely, partially, or not at all, but be aware of the consequences of each choice.
- After you have acted on your intuition, pay attention to the results and record them in your journal. How well did it work out for you? Are you happy you followed your intuition?
- Repeat this exercise regularly and notice how your intuition becomes stronger and more reliable over time.

Using this exercise repeatedly will help you trust your intuition more and more as you see the results of following your gut.

Part 2

Make It a Habit

Habit stacking is a technique that, as we've discussed, helps you form new habits by linking them to existing ones. For example, if you want to start meditating every morning, you can stack it on top of your current habit of brushing your teeth. Here is an exercise to practice habit stacking:

1. Identify a new habit you want to incorporate into your routine.: It should be something simple and specific, such as drinking a glass of water, reading a page of a book, or stretching for five minutes. You might even use the intuition exercise in Part 1 as the habit you want to incorporate daily.
2. Choose an existing habit that you already do every day without fail, such as waking up, having breakfast, or taking a shower. This will be your anchor habit.
3. Write down a sentence that describes how you will stack your new habit on top of your anchor habit. Use the formula: "After I [anchor habit], I will [new habit]." For example, "After I brush my teeth, I will meditate for 10 minutes," or

"After I brush my teeth, I will practice the intuition exercise for 10 minutes."

4. Repeat this sentence to yourself every time you do your anchor habit, then follow through with your new habit. Do this for at least 21 days—this is the average time it takes to form a new habit.
5. Celebrate your success and enjoy the benefits of your new habit. Once the habit is well-established, you can also build upon it. For example, you can extend the time you practice them. Perhaps you go from 10 minutes of meditating to 15, or you gradually increase the reps of a new exercise you do each day.

You can use habit stacking to integrate as many new habits as you need, but you should focus on one at a time. Once one new habit is integrated, then can you move on to the next.

Final Thoughts on Your New Life

Taking off your mask, integrating new, healthier habits into your routine, learning to express gratitude, and building trust in your intuition are all part of developing your new life. As codependents, we've spent our lives trying to please other people, and it can take time to really settle into a habit of prioritizing our own needs. It can be tempting to fall back into the habit of people-pleasing, but once you've become aware of this pattern within yourself, it becomes difficult to ignore when you catch yourself doing it again. It's important to remember that prioritizing your own needs is not a selfish act—it's a necessary act. You can't form healthy relationships with other people until you have a healthy relationship with yourself. That's what freeing yourself from codependency means; you're ready to build that healthy relationship with you. This is one of the most important things you will ever do. That's why, in the next and final chapter, I'll share some thoughts on how you can maintain your budding relationship with you. You'll learn all about keeping it real.

Chapter 10

Keeping It Real

Before I go any further, I want to congratulate you on finding the courage to complete the exercises in this book and seek a new way of living. It's scary to step away from established patterns, even if they no longer serve us. After all, they say, "The devil you know is better than the one you don't." Once we fall into patterns of behavior, it takes strength and courage to break those habits and live differently. You've chosen to do just that, and you should understand just how brave that is and how much strength it took to change your life. But changing your life is exactly what you are doing, so go you!!! I applaud you and feel honored that you have included me in this remarkable accomplishment. I am so proud of you and happy I get to travel with you on this healing journey.

It's a Journey—Not a Destination

You've come a long way indeed, and you need to celebrate that fact, but it is a journey, not a destination. Living with intention and emotional maturity requires ongoing vigilance and self-care as old patterns fade away and new ones emerge. It is crucial to nurture and protect our newfound healthier mindset. Embarking on the journey to heal from codependent patterns is just the beginning of a lifelong pursuit of happiness and fulfillment. It entails prioritizing your own needs and taking the necessary actions to create a satisfying life. The following are a few things to remember on your journey.

Our Partners are Mirrors

Who you choose to be close to says a lot about your relationship with yourself. Choose wisely so you take care of your needs. Ask yourself, what's in this relationship for me? This may sound cynical, but what will this person give you? I don't mean money, I mean will they respect you and grow with you? Or will you leave them behind as they stay stuck in unhealthy patterns? What do they teach you? What do they bring to your new life and mindset? If it isn't positive, maybe they bring you another lesson or gift.

I firmly believe that we attract the right person into our lives at the right time. Each person who comes to you brings a lesson, a gift, but you have to be open to receiving it. Sometimes the gift is difficult to accept, like your codependency, but those who brought the conditions that were right for codependency to develop in you taught you a valuable lesson about loving yourself. They showed you the importance of prioritizing your needs, and now you're on a happier, healthier path for your own future. As you prioritize your own needs and focus on personal growth, you become better equipped to discern the gifts that different partners and important people bring into your life. With this newfound clarity, you can make choices that align with your values and accept the gifts that contribute to your positive growth and development. You know that you don't have to be stuck anymore. You know that you have value and that you deserve love—the *real* kind of love. That is the kind that is giving and supportive, promotes personal growth, and values you for everything you are. With that knowledge, you can finally fly!

Strengthen Your Emotional Maturity

Emotional maturity is the ability to manage one's emotions healthily and constructively. It involves being aware of one's feelings, thoughts, and needs and expressing them appropriately and respectfully. We have worked in many ways on emotional maturity throughout this book. You now have the skills to increase your self-awareness, identify your needs, and express your desires, but that's not all that emotional maturity involves. Emotional maturity also means being able to empathize with others, cope with stress and challenges, and regulate one's impulses and behaviors. You have these skills as well. Some of them you've had all along, whereas others you've learned through the process of healing. You have new coping strategies now, which will help you to regulate your impulses and behaviors appropriately. The most important thing to know about emotional maturity, however, is that it is not something you're born with; rather, it is something that you develop over time through learning and experience. Throughout this book, you've increased your emotional maturity. Here are some things you've learned:

- How to cultivate a realistic and positive self-image.
- How to set healthy boundaries and respect those of others.
- How to communicate clearly and assertively without being overly aggressive or passive.
- How to handle conflicts and disagreements calmly and respectfully.
- How to show gratitude and appreciation for what you have.
- How to express your emotions appropriately and within context.
- How to manage your stress and emotions without resorting to unhealthy coping mechanisms.
- How to seek help and support when needed.

It's important to recognize that emotional maturity is not a static state but an ongoing process that requires continuous effort and growth. It is a multifaceted concept that can vary based on different circumstances and individuals. Therefore, it is important to be mindful of your emotional maturity level and strive to enhance it throughout different aspects of life. Check in with yourself regularly and practice those vital self-care habits to grow your emotional maturity.

Take Responsibility

Finally, the journey you're on requires that you take responsibility for your life. Here's the thing about giving up your codependency habit—it's all up to you now. Now you know that your happiness, self-love, and life are all in your hands. No one else can give you these things; you have to take responsibility for making your life what you want it to be. But that's nothing to worry about. You already know you have the courage to do just that; after all, you picked up this book and ventured on this journey with me. That is an act of courage in and of itself. By embarking on this journey, you've already shown that you are ready for this responsibility. You now have the skills you need to continue growing the strong relationship you've established with yourself. I have no doubt you'll do whatever you decide you need to do going forward. That may mean many things, but from now on, it will always mean that you can take care of yourself with all the love you deserve.

You've Got This

When I first became aware of the depth of my codependency and recognized the need to address it, I was filled with fear and pain. It took that level of pain to make me take a long, hard look at myself and how my trauma had affected me. I knew something was wrong, but I didn't really know what it was. When I saw the reality, I wasn't entirely sure I could change that pattern. As I embarked on my journey of healing, however, my confidence grew daily, and I realized that I could do it. The doubts I had were little more than introjected beliefs haunting the recesses of my mind. I have finally banished those old ghosts, but I continue to work on my personal growth even today. Now, I take pride in guiding others through the darkest corners of their minds toward the light of self-love and self-worth, as I have found in my own life. But even more than that, I'm most happy that I've learned to value myself and insist on getting my needs met. I am truly like that heroic character Ripley, holding my inner child in my arms and conquering any beasts that dare to threaten our inner peace. And so are you!

If I can do this, so can you. What one person can do, so can another. You have the skills, you have a new mindset, and you have a path to follow. Take care of yourself in whatever way that is right for you. Seek out therapy if that's what you feel you need, meditate daily if that speaks to you, continue writing in your journal, take the time to get in touch with your emotions, and most of all, love yourself. Be your own hero because in the end, the one person whom you can be sure you will wake up with every morning for the rest of your life is *you*. So be kind, good, and in love with yourself, and you will find the internal peace that you seek. I know you can do it, and I want to hear all about your success story. Please feel free to contact me at Facebook www.facebook.com/elena.miro.psy and tell me about your heroic journey. Your feedback is so valuable to me, and it only takes one minute of your time to leave a review of this book. I know you're busy, but I love hearing from the people I reach—all the heroes on the same journey I'm on. I believe we are in this life to grow love, and by learning to love yourself, you're contributing to the wellness our world so desperately needs in the modern day. You're helping create a better, more compassionate place for all of us to live. As it turns out, you're not just your own hero; you're a hero for all of us, and to that, I say BRAVO!

References Cited

Co-Dependents Anonymous International. (2022, August 19). CoDA.org. CoDA.org. https://coda.org/.

Diamond, S. A. (2008, June 7). Essential Secrets of Psychotherapy: The Inner Child: Has your adult self spent time with your inner child today? Psychology Today. Retrieved May 23, 2023, from https://www.psychologytoday.com/intl/blog/evil-deeds/200806/essential-secrets-psychotherapy-the-inner-child.

DiPietro JA, Costigan KA, Voegtline KM. Studies In Fetal Behavior: Revisited, Renewed, And Reimagined. *Monogr Soc Res Child Dev*. 2015 Sep;80(3):vii;1-94. doi: 10.1111/mono.v80.3. PMID: 26303396; PMCID: PMC4835043.

Imbir, K.K. (2017). Psychoevolutionary Theory of Emotion (Plutchik). In: Zeigler-Hill, V., Shackelford, T. (eds) Encyclopedia of Personality and Individual Differences. Springer, Cham. https://doi.org/10.1007/978-3-319-28099-8_547-1.

Murray, H. (2023). Transactional Analysis Theory & Therapy: Eric Berne. Simply Psychology. https://www.simplypsychology.org/transactional-analysis-eric-berne.html.

Pantic I. Online social networking and mental health. Cyberpsychol Behav Soc Netw. 2014 Oct;17(10):652-7. doi:

10.1089/cyber.2014.0070. Epub 2014 Sep 5. PMID: 25192305; PMCID: PMC4183915.

Persona – International Association of Analytical Psychology – IAAP. (n.d.). https://iaap.org/jung-analytical-psychology/short-articles-on-analytical-psychology/persona-2/#:~:text=As%20Jung%20says%2C%20%E2%80%9CThe%20persona,true%20nature%20of%20the%20individual.

Siegfried, W. (2014). The Formation and Structure of the Human Psyche: Id, Ego, and Super-Ego – The Dynamic (Libidinal) and Static Unconsciousness, Sublimation, and the Social Dimension of Identity Formation. *Athene Noctua: Undergraduate Philosophy Journal*, 2, 1–3. https://www.fau.edu/athenenoctua/pdfs/William%20Siegfried.pdf.

Van Driel, M. A. (2022, July 12). Projecting the Shadow Self is Surreptitiously Seeing Our Darkness in Others | CPTSDfoundation.org. https://cptsdfoundation.org/2022/07/12/projecting-the-shadow-self-is-surreptitiously-seeing-our-darkness-in-others/.

Venniyoor, A. (2020). PTEN: A Thrifty Gene That Causes Disease in Times of Plenty? *Frontiers in Nutrition*, 7, 81. https://doi.org/10.3389/fnut.2020.00081

www.ingramcontent.com/pod-product-compliance
Lightning Source LLC
LaVergne TN
LVHW010314070526
838199LV00065B/5556